SOME BECOME FLOWERS

ৎ

SOME BECOME FLOWERS

❧

Living with Dying at Home

Sharon Brown

HARBOUR PUBLISHING

Published by:
HARBOUR PUBLISHING
P.O. Box 219
Madeira Park, BC Canada V0N 2H0

Cover photograph and design by Roger Handling

Typeset in Carmina Light. Carmina was designed by Gudrun Zapf-Von Hesse, a German calligrapher born in 1918.

The epigraph by Michael Ignatieff is from *The Needs of Strangers: An essay on privacy, solidarity, and the politics of being human* (Penguin, 1984, p. 15). Quotations by Marguerite Yourcenar are from *Fires* (Farrar, Straus and Giroux, 1981, translated from the French *Feux* by Librairie Plon, 1957, pp. 44, 79 and 100). Quotation by Dennis Lee is from *Alligator Pie*, Macmillan, 1974, p. 8. Quotation by Ferron is from *Shadows on a Dime*, Nemesis Publishing, 1984, Lucy Records, from the song "The Return."

Printed and bound in Canada

Canadian Cataloguing in Publication Data

Brown, Sharon, 1946–
  Some become flowers

  ISBN 1-55017-087-2

  1. Brown, Sharon, 1946–   —Diaries.   2. Brown, Betty.
3. Cancer—Patients—Family relationships.
4. Terminal care—Psychological aspects.
5. Dying—Psychological aspects.
I. Title.
R726.8.B76 1993   362.1'9699471'0092   C93-091650-6

For Andreas, Sabrina, Vanessa,
and also for my father

If we need love, it is for the reasons that go beyond the happiness it brings; it is for the connection, the rootedness, it gives us with others. Most of the things we need most deeply in life—love chief among them—do not necessarily bring us happiness. If we need them, it is to go to the depth of our being, to learn as much of ourselves as we can stand, to be reconciled to what we find in ourselves and in those around us.

ì

Michael Ignatieff, *The Needs of Strangers*

HOMECOMING

❧

2 April 1984

Finally, after three days of driving west from Winnipeg, we pull up to the start of our mountain road. We have just endured eight months of living and working away from home. Our utility trailer, which Andreas welded together out of scrap metal, is packed eight feet high with what we facetiously call "our requirements": books, records, a television, VCR, and microwave; countless toys, musical instruments, a rocking horse, and two cases of wine bought at a great price in Alberta. I have to chuckle inwardly. Our family may be nomadic, but we sure as heck don't have the Bedouin approach. As I unlock the chain at the base of our switchback road, our young daughters, Sabrina and Vanessa, crane their necks the better to hear what I'm calling out to Andreas.

"Figure we should try her?"

Andreas leans out the driver's window to study the road's surface. Silence. We double-check each other's expression. We know full well that the road is never predictable. An absence of ruts at the bottom guarantees nothing about the top, and vice versa. The pit-run gravel at my feet has been gullied into foot-wide scars from this past winter's runoff. It badly needs a layer of crushed rock, but it still looks driveable. Yes. We will chance towing our entire load up in one run. Neither of us wants to stop to unhitch the trailer.

As we drive up I note the newly leafed branches of alders, poplars and maples arching overhead like the vaults of an outdoor cathedral. Salmonberry bushes are already in blossom, and the bleeding hearts and buttercup leaves are encroaching on the shoulder. Our family is wired together in anticipation. Gravel crunches under our tires as we inch our way up. Our truck moves with the inevitability of a full-uddered cow on her way to the milking shed.

By now Andreas is grinning from ear to ear, listening carefully to the sound of the gravel and looking fore and aft simultaneously. If there's been heavy frost heave or runoff, the last turn will be the worst. We ride the corner on the high side. The tires spin and chuff at the washboarded gravel. I am almost dizzy with holding my breath. Then we are past the worst. I exhale forcefully, and match Andreas's foolish grin with one of my own. As we crest the hill I sit up tall and lean forward. There it is, the peak of our roof!

Every time we take a cross-Canada car trip I start the journey as an agnostic, not trusting the highways, the drivers or the big semis that always seem to blare out of nowhere. By the same token, every time we drive up our mountain road after being away a long while, I lack the faith that our house has not been burned to the ground in our absence. As we drove up our road, every inch of my being willed that our house be still intact. Now I can breathe a sigh of relief. It's all there.

As we pass the greenhouse and gardens I hear the first ring of our phone. Maybe it's my friend, Kinga. She had phoned us in Winnipeg four days ago, and had vowed to be the first one to call us when we got home. After eight months away I ache for embraces with old friends, and for feasts of celebration. I bound up the front stairs two at a time, and snag the call on its sixth ring.

It's Mum! Great! I am just like a kid home from the first

day of grade two with a hundred and one things to say and no sense or order in blurting it all out. After five minutes of my snapshot burbling Mum gets a phrase in edgewise.

"So you're just home this minute? Not really?" It's the same "Mum-voice" that used to go with the after-school graham crackers and milk when I was a child. There is profound comfort here. I lean back against the wall savouring our exchange of news.

"So how are things with you and Dad?"

"Well, dear, I'm not so good, it seems. I haven't got the best of news to welcome you home with. I'm so sorry."

I should be cueing in right away, but my attention is diverted by Andreas passing me with an armload of two boxes, the second perched precariously on top of the first.

Mum's next sentence catches me off guard. "Anyway, dear, the doctors have just told me that it looks like I have bone cancer now. It's not been arthritis in my hip as they thought."

Her phrasing is succinct. Normally Mum meanders. Her information updates are usually prefaced with five minutes of chitchat about the ladies at the church or the behaviour of Father's bowels. Her voice gathers momentum now as she proceeds with the details. Her tone is such that she could just as easily be describing a recent bout of flu, or an upcoming dental appointment. I don't know how long, in measurable time, I pause. My body hangs in that empty space before one collapses after being punched in the solar plexus. My mind spins its tires, spewing out a stream of unspoken swear words I blank them out. Even so, my anger over the fact of bone cancer taking root in my mother gives an edge to my response to her.

"Oh, Mum, that's bloody unfair! Shit!"

Two years ago Mum's bladder was removed along with her uterus and ovaries. Her specialist then pronounced that her cure from bladder cancer was complete. At the time of her surgery my father was also weathering major medical storms.

11

He was in another hospital undergoing open heart surgery. It led to complications which precipitated a stroke, a six-week coma, and gangrene which resulted in the amputation of his lower right leg. Once Mum was somewhat recovered, she cared for Dad at home as he stewed in his wheelchair with worsening depressions, aggressions and hallucinations. She even took driving lessons, and earned her first driver's licence in more than twenty years.

This bone cancer means that Mum's initial cancer wasn't actually contained and has already metastasized. Mum describes the progression of her recent symptoms while I continue to grope for words, any words. Finally, when I can speak again, my voice softens.

"You've had enough of that kind of crap."

"I know, dear, but that's the cut of it." She takes a deep breath. "It hasn't been a great winter. Anyway, it wasn't arthritis like my family doctor thought."

"Damn your family doctor. The guy's a regular turkey."

"Well there's really no other choice. The other practices in town were all full when we moved here. We've pretty much got to stick with what we've got. Besides he's not so bad."

"Crumbs, Mum . . . what else does he say? What does this mean? Is there treatment?" I natter on, spinning through a dozen rewordings of the only question: "Is there hope?" We both know and avoid the likely answer.

Andreas walks past with another box to be unloaded in the kitchen. His quizzical look slides into concern at the expression on my face. Mum continues speaking with a seamlessness that suggests she has rehearsed these sentences several times over many cups of tea before she has dared to call.

"Well, dear, I do have to go into Vancouver tomorrow for tests and it will take all day." She reads her schedule of appointments for blood tests, ultrasound, a physical examination and a CAT scan. "They're at three separate addresses but I expect they're in the same block. . . . Anyway, if it's not a bother . . . " I should be responding to this, but I am back to being totally stunned. ". . . I don't know if I should be driving my car into Vancouver, and to do the whole day by taking the bus in might be a bit much because then I'd have to walk in from Harris Road at the end of the day, but don't worry if you're busy, dear . . . ."

The walk from her home to Harris Road and the Lougheed Highway is more than a mile. The bus ride into town requires three transfers that involve long waits at connection points that don't have shelter. That she could even consider this as an option shakes me loose.

"Please, Mum. Don't even think of the bus. Of course I'll drive you in. Andreas can mind the kids." We quickly work out the remaining details and slide back into formula, back into our habitual ways with telephone talk and goodbyes.

We both know, without needing to say so, that we are just starting to take in the news that she is dying and we are simultaneously scared, angry and grieving. Home now for only fifteen minutes, I pace around unsettled. I don't know where to put myself. I feel like an emotional chemistry experiment where the addition of one element changes the nature of all the others. I am still glad to be home, yet it is as if this particular joy is now being held in suspense. Andreas hugs me briefly, but I move away to continue my pacing, and to rehearse in my mind the required events of the next few days.

What will Mum need? What will Dad need? What can I give? I stare unseeing through the living room window. How can I balance all this with the needs of the children and Andreas? Life is a juggling act as it is without this. Can I do it? I walk blankly through the kitchen, my hand skiffing over a row of boxes on the table. Mum's needs will be immense. She is dying. I suddenly feel so small, so weak, so pale; I feel like a child needing her mother. Damn it all, this is so unfair for her, for all of us.

I come back into the living room and sit heavily on the

sofa. Andreas sits down to embrace me. My lone tear glistens on his down vest. The kitchen table is covered with unpacked boxes. He has already half unloaded the truck. Sabrina and Vanessa are rediscovering their old swing set and sandbox in the back yard. There is work to be done, but for the moment Andreas and I stare out at the hemlocks and cedars, and breathe in the welcome mix of wood smoke, cedar and mountain air.

FLASHBACK

ė

8 November 1982

On the day of my thirty-sixth birthday, a year and a half before Mum's phone call, I took our youngest daughter Vanessa into hospital. She was two months old and was vomiting on a regular basis, not just the usual infant spit-ups. The force with which she vomited was frequently enough to hit unsuspecting targets six feet away. We feared dehydration; often she wasn't getting enough fluids to dampen her diaper. We went into the hospital suspecting something like pyloric stenosis, a condition where a malfunction of a valve at the base of the stomach doesn't permit food to proceed along its natural course. That didn't prove to be the case.

Vanessa and I stayed at British Columbia's Children's Hospital in Vancouver for three days. While the soap operas blared continuously from the overhead televisions in our ward, I passively endured the finale of one Hollywood drama after another. Unlike their scripts, my own life was pointedly on hold. Vanessa underwent X-rays, ultrasound and a battery of blood tests, but I was told nothing about their results. The hospital timetable led us to no truth or understanding. Every speck of Vanessa's urine, feces and vomit were weighed and recorded. Feed times and amounts were noted with metric precision. Flurries of whitecoats flocked at our door, rustling and whispering, but still telling me nothing.

After all their tests, Vanessa was given a label: she had been born with Delange Syndrome. Cornelia Delange to be precise. The pediatrician said she would likely be profoundly retarded and stunted in growth, and would have a much shorter than average life span. Some Delange babies lived till their teens. Half of them died before age two. For those who survived, there were often major behavioural problems. No one knew why, but these children had a harder time reaching out. There was a high likelihood of autism.

Fifteen minutes after I received this bombshell, Vanessa woke crying for her nursing. I sat on the window ledge about five feet away thinking, "Why bother?" My own voice had never echoed so remotely, sounded so dead, inside myself. For a moment or two my breaths were forced, as if thick bands constrained my chest. I stared fixedly past the window at the treetops beneath. Then, without any conscious decision, somehow I was by her crib, reaching out, and she was in my arms, first seeking a breast, then sucking rhythmically. As my milk let down, so did my relief, and I showered the bared skin of her upraised arm with tears and a sudden spurt of excess milk.

In the months that followed, Andreas and I served our apprenticeship on how to handle the medical system to good advantage. We learned how to endure endless months of fractured sleep, and learned the realities of that old adage: that which doesn't kill you makes you strong. I thought that I had learned all I needed to know about rage and grief and love in my adolescence, but I learned that I had only just begun.

When I relive those days, I can still feel my jaw set in anger at the shortfalls of our overall medical and social systems. I will never forget the pinched face of Jason's mother, the only mother besides me who spent her nights in our ward at Children's Hospital. Her son had been born with his intestines outside his body; although that problem had been surgically repaired, Jason wasn't "thriving." His eyes were sunken. His face was that of a wizened old man. During the three months that Jason's mother had been staying with him, her husband had left her. She couldn't keep up the rent on their apartment and didn't know what would happen next. She was nineteen years old. She had no visitors. Part of her hoped her baby would die. This woman and her child taught me a lot about the costs of commitments that are violated, and the way that our culture abandons people who are resourceless. This experience shook me out of my middle class complacency that all problems have solutions.

OUR FIRST TRIP

ع

5 April 1984

I speed down Highway 7 to Pitt Meadows, to pick up Mum for her full slate of medical appointments. It's the first of many such trips. It is not quite eight o'clock in the morning. I jam the last crust of toast into my mouth and suck the crumbs off my fingers. I'm a little taken aback at how happy I feel, given the reason for this trip. It must have something to do with the joy of being back home, back on the west coast. Silvermere Lake glistens to my right, the Fraser River to my left. After a winter stuck in the slums of Winnipeg with a one-year-old and a four-year-old, this time alone is true luxury. My fingers bang out the rhythms of a Joan Armatrading song on the steering wheel of the Rabbit.

I arrive at Mum's and Dad's at a quarter to nine. I'd really enjoy a cup of coffee, but I decide not to complicate life. Dad is seated in his wheelchair, wearing his turquoise hospital gown and watching the *Canada AM* show. When he came home from hospital a couple of years ago, he ordered half a dozen hospital gowns for home use. He claims that they are practical, but I think that he needs to feel like a patient. He wears them half the day. Mum asks if I'd like a "cuppa char," but I decline.

"Finish yours, Mum. We're not in a rush." I slump, suddenly weary, onto the chesterfield. There is something about being with both my parents that always leaves me gasping for emotional air like a fish out of water. I can never put my finger on it. I feel unevolved, as if my emotional gills haven't adapted enough for me to filter out their sludge and still absorb enough air. We talk for a few moments over the blare of the television, past Father who has barely acknowledged my presence. He is working hard to keep me tuned out, as if I am some kind of static. This quietly infuriates me. He might wonder how I've been after a year away. I ask him how he is. Silence. There's a game going on here that I don't want to play.

Clearly he is not going to say anything, although I sense that Mum wants him to. Part of me is curious about what was said before I got there. Do I dare to dig? Probably not. When it comes to emotional spadework with my parents, I'm a devout coward. Mum, after a few more moments of stilted conversation, stands up and grabs her cane. With brittle chirpiness she announces, "We'd best be off." She is obviously in pain, but shrugs off all help as she eases into the Rabbit.

As I drive she catches me up on all the family goings-on. Apparently my middle brother Struan and his wife Sarah are still running their greenhouse business on the side. Struan is getting good full-time hours at the mill, but the union is readying for a fight and he doesn't know if the company will lock out for the summer. My oldest brother Brian, just two years younger than me, seems to be enjoying his work as a log broker and is probably making pots of money.

"Though goodness knows," Mum adds, "he earns it."

The family vignettes spin out, in no particular order, like knots on a thread marking the length of my time away. Martin, my youngest brother, and his girlfriend Paige were up just last week visiting Mum and Dad. Paige brought a fresh fruit salad for them, and Martin showed them the latest electric guitar that he'd made.

"Pink," Mum says. "When you turn it sideways in the

stage lights it looks red. Can you feature that? A young man from a band called Loverboy—you've heard of them?—is apparently going to buy it." She shakes her head in puzzled but proud amazement, and begins her update on my second-youngest brother Bruce.

During the daytime Bruce works long hours as a plumber, then at night either practises music or plays bar gigs with his and Martin's band. Mum frets about him. He's so good with the children and helping with the cooking and such, but the hours are so long. Both he and his wife Colleen work full time. Still, Mum accepts all that we do and are. Like a list on the fridge, this inventory of her four sons, their wives and children flows on with ease. I wear my mother's presence like a comfortable old coat.

She tells a story of Struan and Sarah's daughter, three-year-old Iris, asking big brother Conde, aged five, "Conde, how you get boobs?" Conde had authoritatively told her, "You gotta be good else you don't get 'em." Later that afternoon, when Sarah had the two kids out shopping, a large-bosomed woman was in the checkout lineup ahead of them. Mum starts chuckling in anticipation of the punch line. "'Wow!' Iris piped up in her voice that could be heard all the way to the meat counter. 'Look at those boobs! Is she ever good!'" Not that Mum hasn't told me the story before, but it fills the time, it's safe to tell, and we enjoy our shared chuckle. Mum is not about to talk about her bone cancer. Fair enough.

There is no parking close to the British Columbia Cancer Agency; the whole block is in the throes of a major addition and renovation. I let Mum off at the appropriate door, where she is greeted by a doorman and helped inside to a chair. His old world courtliness triggers optimism. I rejoin Mum after parking a couple of blocks away, and together we navigate the indoor equivalent of a city block. The entire hallway is undergoing reconstruction. We step over extension cords and sections of missing floor tile. We carefully edge past piles of plywood and wallboard. My optimism evaporates. In the midst of all this debris are the people who await treatment. They lie on the dozens of stretchers lined up in the hallways. It's hard to know where or how to look. It's like coming on someone naked who isn't a close friend or family member. Mothers wait with their pale and balding children, their faces blank with pain. Miracles are needed in these halls.

"I couldn't bear that," says my mother. "Not for my own children."

Finally we arrive at the appropriate treatment station. Mum collapses into the first available chair, and hands me her medical card and appointment slip. I convey them both to the clerk, who looks quizzical and asks for Mum's "Cancer Control Clinic Record of Visits."

"Her what?"

This card, it seems, has to be stamped each time before patients can be seen. Nobody told us this. We should have picked it up at the front office near the door where we came in. Fortunately we are early. Mum hands me her purse with anything in it that I might need, and I retrace my steps back through the labyrinth. I start to hear the warning roars of my inner she-tiger, the same roars I heard when Vanessa was at Children's Hospital. I growl under my breath. One more shot of bureaucracy and I'll come unleashed.

When I get back with the appropriate card, Mum is waiting in a stark white cubicle wearing nothing but a white nightie and a brave wan smile. We have begun the diagnostic ritual that will repeat itself regularly over the next half year. I sit down beside her and she pats my knee.

"You'll get used to it," she says. "It's a special kind of torture that is inflicted upon the sick. You arrive, then wait. Then go to an empty closet, take your clothes off, and wait. Then you dress, go to another department, and wait. Find another closet, take off your clothes, wait, and so on . . . ." She turns her palms face up and shrugs.

After the morning appointments we lunch at the White Spot, where Mum has her usual tea and toast and I pig out on the full hamburger platter, only to spend the afternoon burping pickles. We make the mistake of assuming that her CAT scan is in the same building as the Radiology Department. It turns out to be another half-block down the hill and around the corner. I curse myself for not checking it all out ahead of time. My anger barometer rises. They, the ubiquitous "they," could have given us a map, for goodness' sake. A great ruddy hike is not what a person with a cancerous thigh bone needs! Since the scan will take about an hour once it is started and they are running half an hour late, we agree that I will use the time to run downtown, pick up some Murchie's coffee and stop in at Duthie Books.

When I return an hour and a half later, Mum still isn't finished. Her CAT scan has to be redone. She had suggested to a nurse that her ostomy hardware might have to be removed, that it might interfere with the picture. The nurse had assured her it would be no problem. Wrong again. It takes another three quarters of an hour to redo. Growl. We have been at this now for seven hours. Seven hours! I fret that with rush hour traffic it will take another two hours before I can get her home.

"Well, as long as *you* go to the bathroom, we'll be okay," Mum quips, making a joke of her ostomy gear. I collect her purse and sweater and hand her her cane. In spite of her bravado, her fatigue is showing as she heads for the door independently, with a staccato lurch of a walk. "Jeez, Mum. Walk like that and they'll be running one more test on you—a breathalyser test!" I tease her in the hopes that she'll take my arm for support. She takes it with a mock grimace.

As we drive home, she describes the whole CAT scan process to me. "It's science fiction. Really." She straightens her purse in her lap, and her hands gesture the shape of the machinery. ". . . dozens and dozens of little parts, you can't imagine what they're all good for. It took its own good time, taking pictures every half inch or so." She leans over conspiratorially. "It's bad enough for me. Think what your father would have been like if they had to CAT scan him!" She pauses, waiting for my chuckle. My father is a good foot taller than my mother and shorter by a long shot in the patience department.

Mum's ability to deflect the assaults of the day amazes me. Maybe she always had this skill, or maybe she developed it as a survival tool living with my father, having two children in her thirties, then a miscarriage, then three children in her forties. All that and moving every year from one air force base to another. As a kid I went to twelve different schools, but at the time I never stopped to think about what that might mean to her. I should be sharing these reflections with her, but it doesn't occur to me until later, when I have already dropped her off at her home.

Neither of us has learned the art of getting easily to the nub of real talk with each other. I know this, but it doesn't change how I act with her. Later I wonder out loud to Andreas that maybe she'll die with the two of us not really sharing what matters and being strangers to each other in so many corners of our lives.

KNOWING MY MOTHER

ك

April 1981

The time when I felt closest to my mother, adult to adult, began when I stayed with her for the two weeks following her bladder surgery. It was in April 1981, three years before her bone cancer. I had flown in from our temporary home in Regina to stay with her at her and Dad's home till she got on her feet. Sabrina, who was still nursing then, had come with me. Dad was still at St. Paul's Hospital. Just out of a six-week coma, he looked for all the world like a great beached whale. Grey. Massive. Helpless.

That first night Mum and I had the devil of a time sorting out all the new ostomy gear and hooking it up to the overnight container. As with so many new appliances, the directions and pictures on the package bore little resemblance to the kinds of tubing that had to be fitted together to make it all work. Each new attempt at solving this puzzle deepened our camaraderie. After an hour of wrong tries we finally got it right, and collapsed onto their king-sized bed feeling smug in our victory.

We lay together in the dark, talking with the fresh familiarity of young women on an overnight camp-out. Mum described all the recent "foofaraw" of Dad's medical crises. After Dad had spent six weeks in a coma with no brain activity showing on the monitors, Brian had signed the documents to disconnect Dad's life support systems. Death was what we had all expected, but the result was life. With a few great shuddering heaves Dad's body had decided to breathe for itself. Now that he could eat and talk, and was increasingly able to remember, Mum had hopes that he would walk again. She made plans to regain her driver's licence so she could drive him. Even so, she was still angry with Brian for giving approval to disconnect Dad's life supports without even asking her. Playing devil's advocate, I argued in Brian's defence.

"Yeah, but Mum, he did it because he thought you weren't quite there yourself. Maybe he should have checked with you, but he was trying to protect you too." Mum responded with another rehash of her anger. Since this topic was beginning to spin its tires, we shifted course slightly. She puzzled over Brian, her eldest son. How different he was from her. When her bladder cancer and Dad's coma struck, Brian always wanted to believe the bleakest picture.

"Why," she implored, "must he always insist that the bad side of things is the only side there is? Why expect the worst when there is still room for hope? We're going to come out of this. Look how far your father has come already. And I'm going to be fine, too." By now we were both starting to fade. My jet lag was taking its toll, and this seemed like a good note to fall asleep on. I patted her shoulder, she squeezed my hand. I don't really know who fell asleep first.

The next morning, Sabrina tiptoed in from the guest room where she had been sleeping. She was one-and-a-half years old, jam-packed full of toddler impishness, and good with words beyond her years. Like a performing puppet, she bobbed her head up at the foot of our bed, and recited her favourite poem, "Six little mice sat down to spin . . . ." When she came to the last line, "That may be so, but you don't come in," her little index finger stabbed the air with mock authority.

Mum started as if she had seen a ghost, albeit a friendly one. "Did you know that was the first poem that you decided to memorize? You would have been about the same age. Her voice is yours exactly. Same inflection." She paused. "I could have closed my eyes and been back thirty-five years."

Sabrina goofed around at the foot of the bed, oblivious to our astonishment. Suddenly she made a quick dash to the toilet and we heard pee tinkling in the bowl. She returned instantly.

"Did you wipe?"

"Yep. Can I come in?"

"Sure, but easy, eh? You've got to be gentle." My maternal cautions, always at the ready, were ignored as usual. Sabrina bounded onto the bed, batting me inadvertently with her bear, and then commando-crawled over my body to snuggle up between me and Mum. She pulled the covers up under her chin and giggled, shaking her legs in delight. First she shot a loving grin toward Mum, then she turned toward me and patted my breast. Once fed she snuggled down with Bear and thumb, her flashing blue eyes following every turn of our conversation.

Mum and I spent the next half-hour talking about what it is like to be a mother when children are young. "You know there were times when I just don't know how I did it all. When your father was at Cold Lake on training, and Martin was just three months old, and Bruce was barely fourteen months, I had to get our whole house packed for storage. I didn't know what to pack for France, what to leave behind. I don't know what I would have done without you."

"I don't know how you did it either, Mum. I can't imagine. Five kids, moving to France, and all that. Don't know if I could hack it." In the pauses, between topics, I glowed in her praise. I wasn't that bad a kid. I was her Sabrina, her first-born. Her only daughter. Now I knew what that meant. Tucked in together this morning, the three of us so closely mothers and daughters, I felt Mum's essence inside my own skin as I often felt Sabrina's. Finally, nudged by Sabrina's urgings, we broke the magic, got up and found some cheerios for Bear.

Regrettably the easy familiarity of that time evaporates when Dad is around. Perhaps all of Mum's energies are spent on surveillance, on defusing our family land mines and on steering us all to safety. But maybe, too, there is another explanation. How much of Mum's self-snuffing has to do with the predictable tangles that Dad and I are so good at triggering together? Maybe Mum can only find the room to be herself when she only has to contend with the needs of one of us at a time.

ROUTINE DEPRESSIONS

؟

23 April 1984

Today Mum is scheduled for her first radiation treatment, although she is still not entirely sure about even having them. I'm not sure either. I am unclear about how these treatments will help. I raise questions to which there are no answers. Mum is caught in a tug of war between my cynicism, and Dad's optimism about the effectiveness of Big Time Medicine. I want Mum to have the freedom to make *her* choice. At the same time, I know full well that she will probably defer to the authority of the doctors and my father. She always has.

Over the past three years, Mum hasn't made any of the lifestyle changes that have been recommended in order to reduce her risks of recurrence. She did exercise for a little while with a set of weights that she made out of tins of vegetables tied up inside old pantyhose. She progressed from doing ten lifts with one can tied around each ankle to doing twenty lifts with two cans, and then she quit because she felt so much better. Her diet probably hasn't helped much either, but it has only been quite recently that our great North American diet has proven to be so toxic. Old habits die hard. I also suspect that what makes it even harder is that Mum has also been afflicted for a long time with a chronic low-level depression that sucks away the basic vitality needed to initiate change. This is not surprising. The only time that I see it lift is in Dad's absence. Anytime Dad goes into hospital Mum blossoms: visits her children's families, plays with her grandchildren. Something similar, but on a smaller scale, also happens to Dad. When Mum is in hospital he is a little less morose. Together they undermine one another and reinforce each other's weaknesses. No wonder she has never leapt onto a table and yelled, "Carpe diem!"

We have driven into Vancouver twice since the CAT scan, once to meet a therapeutic oncologist, and once for her to be tattooed so the radiologist will have an accurate target for administering the radiation. The day she got home after being tattooed, she flounced into the living room to greet Father, "I've just been tattooed. Makes me a more interesting woman." Her gift for turning tragedy on its nose is still intact.

I expect to be depressed by our trip to the radiation department but am pleasantly surprised. Many of the clientele are clearly veterans. They know the receptionist, the doctors and the technicians; many of them know each other well enough to inquire about books read and grandchildren. Most of the patients are Mum's age, although there is one little boy about eighteen months old with blistered arms and a dauntingly pale face. Vanessa tries to entice him to play, but his mother yells at him to sit still, not whimper and shut up. She looks no more than a teenager. Her black-leather-jacketed arms cross grimly in front of her breasts, and shield her in her isolation and rage. Daunted, Vanessa retreats and clings to my leg.

Mum has asked me to come in during the talk with her oncologist, although he would obviously prefer to deal with her alone. She has written down her questions about side-effects, and asks me to read them. She can't read without her glasses which are back in the booth with her clothes. Her list questions whether her hair will fall out, and raises the possibility of diarrhea, abdominal pain and nausea.

"There will be no side-effects whatsoever from the radiation," he assures us. "That's an unfounded concern left over from the early days when dosages were higher." Our polite faces mask our incredulity. "The only negative side-effect that you might experience is some constipation from the effects of the morphine. For that, you might like to try different laxatives until you find which one is best for you."

Vanessa keeps opening forbidden drawers full of intriguing shiny steel tools and it takes half my attention just to keep her out of trouble. The doctor has no answers for our questions and we are overstaying our welcome. He seems bored with the whole process, eager to get on to the next billable cog. I start to feel as though I am in a slowed-down black-and-white film with the sound turned off. The rub of the system is lethal. I feel frustrated, angry and impotent, and feel that I am profoundly betraying the needs of my mother. Even so, I am incapable of doing anything more than taking my leave. The guns of my anger are trained on myself. I fold up Mum's list, help her to her feet and haul Vanessa off the examining table.

"It's all right, dear," Mum says, comforting me as Vanessa and I walk her down the hallway toward her first treatment, "I think it's the right thing to do." When I should be the one offering the mothering, I am still the kid, the one being comforted.

27 April 1984

Mum has had five treatments this week. A volunteer driver took her in the other four times. Although Vanessa usually threw up at least once as we drove home from the cancer clinic, and the four-hour round trips were wearing me out, I really avoided this contribution of driving Mum in because of my own depression. We are getting nowhere. We are just feeding one more dying and diseased victim to a medical monster that is growing fatter daily. I am angry at my complicity. I feel sapped and want no more of it. I am angry at baldfaced lies from doctors. In spite of the oncologist's assurances, Mum is stricken with unrelenting diarrhea. My family doctor tells me that he has never heard of anyone who didn't get diarrhea after radiation.

"I guess the trouble is that the oncologists never see the GP's end of things. It's a different story for sure than what they preach," he says. "The good bacteria that thrive in the mucosa in your mother's gut are likely trashed. Possibly acidophilus or yoghurt could help."

30 April 1984

I phone our family doctor again. Mum has been battling constant nausea for the past week. I have talked to various friends, including a naturopath, and a friend's parents who have played the medical cancer game for the past seven years. All agree that the only likely help is marijuana. One of my brothers gets some for me—premium bud, I am told—and I find Alice B Toklas's recipe for "Haschich Fudge (which anyone could whip up on a rainy day)." Good old Alice B. Toklas. The cookbook cautions: "Euphoria and brilliant storms of laughter; ecstatic reveries and extensions of one's personality on several simultaneous planes are to be complacently expected. Almost anything Saint Theresa did, you can do better if you can bear to be ravished by 'un evanouissement reveille.'"

I'm not sure that my mother can "bear to be ravished" by anything at this time in her life. I do emphasize to her how important it is to mix the dope in with the butter. Otherwise it globs in lumps and gets spread unevenly. Things could get wild. I sense her hesitation as we talk, so hasten to add that maybe the simplest option is to steep it in tea. Never know the difference. I am at least not dumb enough to suggest smoking it.

7 May 1984

Mum's hair has thinned but she is too spent to get it cut and cared for. Her abdominal pain, an intermittent torment for months, has become constant. It seems her rage has turned inwards. A deepening depression robs her of the little corners of delight that she has formerly been capable of creating for herself. Dad regularly gets angry with her because she won't eat. He phones me to complain and tries to enlist my help in bullying her to start eating.

"She sat in front of a lovely piece of sole with a butter dill sauce for supper, and wouldn't take a bite. She is not being reasonable. How the heck are we going to knock some sense into her head? I end up eating it all. What's that good for?"

I fend him off as best I can, but it's a series of sorry scenes. I feel soiled by the whole experience. I confine my help to the weekly or biweekly trips to doctors, clinics or ostomy supply stores. Daily homemaker service helps clean their house, do the laundry and start their meals, which Dad then eats for both of them. As much as I can, I shove their needs out of mind, plant and tend my own garden, take time with Vanessa and Sabrina, and cook just for us. The weeks drag slowly.

MOTHER'S DAY

❦

13 May 1984

We all turn up at Mum's and Dad's with the unvoiced feeling that this will be Mum's last Mother's Day. We desperately want the day to be special not only for us, but for her. We're all walking on eggs, doing our damnedest to stay out of trouble with Dad. It is possible that Mum could have done without the whole kit and caboodle of us visiting in one fell swoop. In the past, Mother's Day has never attracted this kind of attention. A phone call and a card have usually sufficed. Maybe flowers and things made by the grandchildren. Today it is obvious what our collective presence here implies. Twenty-one of us are shoehorned into Mum's and Dad's modest co-op quarters: four sons and their wives, Andreas and I, and nine grandchildren aged from six months to ten years.

I am called away to deal with a crisis. While I was setting out food, Vanessa got into Dad's nitroglycerine pills. They are spilled all over the bedroom carpet and one pill is wet with spit. I hope that she tried just one and then spat it out. Her mouth shows no traces. I count out the remaining pills; four short of the full prescription.

"Dad, Vanessa got into these. Do you know how many you've used?"

"Who the hell let the little bitch at them?"

"I don't know, Dad. Someone left the bedroom door open." Damn him, anyway! This is not the issue. "How many have you used?"

"Maybe two. Maybe three."

"Shit," I think to myself. She may have eaten one or two. I call our family doctor. "What should I do? What symptoms should I look for?"

When I return to the living room, Mum is slumped in an armchair. Seated on the arms of the chair are two granddaughters: Ingrid and Korina. Mikolt is taking a picture of the three of them. Mum's face is lined with pain and weighted with resignation. Her ankles are swollen and her body, which has gotten heavier over the past decade, looks not only heavy but slack. Her gaze looks down below the lens of the camera that captures the moment. On the back of the picture will be written "Mother's Day, 1984." I don't know whose day it is, but it sure doesn't feel like *her* day.

The banter that we are all generally known for, the awful puns and questionable jokes, are all falling flat. Dad is irritable, but this is nothing new. All our lives he has been irritable, and during the past few months he has been taking his anger over Mum's illness out on her. She is still massaging the stump where he lost part of his leg to gangrene and washing his body daily. "The homemakers never do it right," he says. "Scrub my ass like they were scouring a roasting pan." Once Martin did it for him, but I refuse. There are limits.

We silently loathe Dad for his treatment of Mum, but arguing with him always rebounds on her, so we have given up. It's his way of exerting control. Once when I was thirteen and had been disobedient, just after he'd decided that I was too old to hit, he threw Brian clear across the kitchen to land in a heap by the fridge. "Does that show you something, missy?" he had demanded. It was an effective blackmail. Andreas bounces Vanessa on his knee. She doesn't look pale or sweaty, the symptoms we have been warned about. We got lucky, I guess.

Struan carefully places Dad's tea on the knitted coaster, on his left side, one inch in from the edge of the side-table. Even today had Struan not been here, Mum would have made Dad his tea. Struan is the least likely to get into trouble for blowing it, and most readily forgiven if he does. If one of the rest of us had made the tea, it would have been all wrong. Dad would have had to yell at us for failing to add the exact proportions of sweetener and milk, or else for putting the cup down in a manner designed to enrage him. We treat him like nitroglycerine.

On the drive home my eyes well up and I vent my outrage to Andreas. "It isn't fair. On top of the cancer, she has to kowtow to the 'Master.' Shit. He takes care of himself just fine when she isn't there. Bastard treats us all like bloody dingbats!" I pause for a few moments and focus on the rapid swipes of the windshield wipers.

"Jesus, Schroeder! How does he keep getting away with it? Why? Why does she let him do it?" I want so much to take her home and offer the care that she deserves. She won't come, though. Not unless he agrees, and he never will. She's his caretaker, come hell or high water, and as long as she can put one foot in front of the other, she will wait on him to the end.

POINT AND COUNTERPOINT: PART ONE

❧

4 June 1984

Mum has been in hospital in Maple Ridge since May 24. She was admitted with severe abdominal pain, and all the doctors can find is that her electrolytes are all out of whack. A week earlier she took a taxi to emergency but was sent home with a diagnosis of flu. Now she is wearily explaining to me that there is nothing new to add to the explanations of what's happening and that she doesn't really know what any of her symptoms mean. I allow as how I don't either.

"Heck. I don't know if I'd recognize an electrolyte if I saw one waltzing toward me," I say. Mum squeezes my hand, appreciative of my attempts at humour. "Should I try and find out what an electrolyte is?"

"No. It doesn't matter."

"Guess not. If it made any sense, they'd tell you."

"Ha!" The depth of her cynicism catches me short.

This is one of many visits when I have Sabrina and Vanessa in tow. Fortunately Sabrina loves hospitals and she wants to know what everything is and how it works. She also knows how to charm answers out of passing orderlies and nurses. After all, her Mum isn't any good at her incessant questions such as why anyone needs saline, or how come the man in the next room moans so much. Just now she has followed a nurse to find out how they get stuff into needles. Thank goodness there's usually one nurse around who's prepared to countenance such curiosity. Vanessa, thankfully, was napping when we arrived. I have parked the car in the shade just beneath Mum's window where I can still keep an eye on her. The other two patients in Mum's room are snoring energetically, and the third bed is empty.

"Mrs. MacKenzie went home this morning because her blood pressure was doing ever so much better," Mum says. She has told me during previous visits that Mrs. MacKenzie is in the Eastern Star, and that they used to roll bandages together for cancer patients. Since I've heard all this before I am only half tuned in. "It was nice having her here," Mum natters on. This is cake-decorating talk: sweet, and smooth, and designed to cover the surface. I go over to the window to peek at Vanessa, peacefully sleeping in her car seat, pink cheeked, with her head resting easily on her left shoulder. Sabrina is still with the nurse.

Times like this are rare. I don't know when the next chance for private conversation will be, so decide that it is time to do more than just chat. The chairs and beds are all the wrong angles for good conversation but there's no changing that. I sit down on a chair low enough to put my chin only slightly higher than Mum's elbow, and stroke her hand.

"What do *you* think is happening here, Mum? I mean aside from all this electrolyte stuff."

"I don't know, dear. I still can't eat without ending up feeling awful. Your father's been most upset with me. And I've just got no energy. None at all." Then suddenly with an uncharacteristic whimper and crack in her voice: "This is awful, being here."

"God, I know. I hate it too. . . . Is this where you want to be? Do you feel like you're being helped?"

"There isn't any choice, sweetie. I can't go home. We only have the homemaker for one hour a day, and I can't wash father, or cook, or anything. . . . Not just now . . . ."

"No, I didn't figure that. But I could take you home to my place—that is, if you'd like—and care for you there. The boys could bring Dad up to visit so he wouldn't feel left out. It's not like he comes here that often anyway, maybe once a week."

"Thank you, dear, but no, I couldn't do that to you. You've got enough on your plate."

"Well, it's worth a try. We could work something else out if it got to be too much. It might even add up to the same amount of time, whether I spend it driving here or to Vancouver, or helping you in my own home. Actually, I'd rather spend time with you at home than here, if that counts for anything."

I know that the only way that she will leave the hospital and come home with me, no matter how badly she wants to, will be if she believes that such a choice would be helpful. She is fearful of ever being a burden to anyone. She hasn't been accustomed in her life to thinking about what *she* might need or want. Now that I've put the home care option into words for the first time, the idea makes even more sense to me than when it just rattled around quietly in my head. Just thinking of all the long drives for awkward visits that I have already made and have yet to make suggests that having her stay with us might not be so crazy. Mum rests quietly for a moment with the thought.

"You know, Mum, sometimes I think it might be easier without all these around." I gesture at the snoring bodies of the two sick people whom I don't even know, and by whom I suddenly feel invaded. At least, I think to myself, Mrs. MacKenzie has gone. She was always such a chatterer that Mum and I felt like a sideshow. I used to resent driving for three-quarters of an hour to spend most of my time listening to Mrs. MacKenzie.

"Well, maybe I'll get better soon, and go home." We both take a moment to turn the likelihood of this over in our minds, each of us silent.

"Okay, Mum, but what about when it gets to . . . well, when it gets to when you're not going to get better, what do you want us to do then?" This is hard, and I am stumbling, feeling myself getting all formal, stiff, dangerously far from how I want to say all this. Mum reaches for her purse, opens it, but doesn't find what she is looking for. She pats my hand as though it is "never any mind." "Well, anyway, your father and I have worked that all out. No heroic measures. We've got that on our doctors' records. And I don't want any more radiation or chemotherapy or any of that."

"I agree," I sigh, "Yes, that makes sense." I pause for a moment wondering if I should go further. "But what about when it comes time for dying, Mum? We need to know about that. Where do you want to be?" Mum fingers the sheet folds. I continue, having braved it this far and not wanting to lose momentum.

"Remember the awful time when Dad was taken off the respirator? Brian sure took a lot of flak on that one, and God knows I have a hard time seeing it his way, but he was only trying to do what he thought best."

"Well, he should have asked me."

"You were still weak from your bladder surgery, and Dad for sure was beyond asking at that point. Mum," I implore, "I want to do better by you this time around."

Mum grabs my hand and holds on tightly while her voice is suddenly frail and barely audible. "I don't want to die in a hospital."

"You don't have to die in a hospital!" My voice is more insistent than I intend. "You could come and stay at our house, you know. Andreas and I have talked it over. We figure that we could handle it. We want to, if it's what you want. Our doctor says that he'd give us backup, home visits and such, and he's great. I've got lots of friends who say that they'd help me out with the kids. You can choose it if you want it."

"I don't know what your father would say," she back-pedals.

"It's *your* life, Mum. Please! It's your life."

At this point Sabrina bursts in full of chatter about her discoveries. As a diversion, I ask her to look out the window to see if Vanessa still naps. I am sure she does, but I need a bit more undiverted time myself. While Sabrina drags a chair over and clambers up to look over the window ledge, I stay holding my mother's hand in silence.

"Yep. She's still asleep, Mum." Sabrina brings the chair back and climbs up very gingerly beside my mother. "I want to get into bed with Grandma."

"No, sweetheart. Grandma's pretty sick and needs some rest, but you can stay here while I just go and talk with the nurses to see if there's any news to take back to Grampa."

There isn't. The nursing station staff check their schedules and report that the doctor will be doing his rounds early in the evening. I walk down to the end of the hall to a pay phone to call Dad and tell him this. When I come back, Sabrina is nowhere to be seen. I'm sure my displeasure is written big all over my face because Mum puts a finger to her lips, smiles at me to calm down, and points beneath the bed. Sure enough, there she is—hiding. I feel rubbed the wrong way, and all of a sudden quite leaden with fatigue.

"Come on, sweetheart, we have to go."

"No."

"YES!"

"I want to stay with Grandma."

"I do, too, but Vanessa's going to wake up soon, and I can't stand driving back to Mission with her screaming and throwing up all over the place, so we're going now."

"That's not fair, Mum. I want to sleep here with Grandma tonight. You could get me tomorrow? It's not right, Mum, and you're not fair." She clings to the bedpost.

My fatigue begets rigidity. I kiss Mum, say I'll see her in a couple of days, yank Sabrina from under the bed, tell her that she can kiss Grandma goodbye and then we are leaving. "No arguments, please." On the way out, the excitement of being able to punch the elevator buttons distracts her. I feel the easing cold of the metal elevator wall as I lean against it all the way down.

On the way home, Sabrina revives her contested point. "You know you were mean, Mum. It's not nice to leave Grandma all alone when she's sick."

"I know, dear. It's not fair, but that's how it is sometimes. The hospital doesn't let little kids stay over. You were doing the right thing." I look at her in the rear view mirror, knees up to her chest, sucking her thumb with a well-worn teddy bear paw snugged up against her nose. "Maybe Grandma will come home and stay with us. Then you could help take care of her."

"I'd like that," she mumbles over her thumb.

POINT AND COUNTERPOINT: PART TWO

ع

5 June 1984

At eight in the evening the phone rings, and I know it's Dad.

"What's all this I hear about you trying to talk Mother into staying at your house?" This is not a question but a declaration that his patriarchal rights have been trampled on.

I sag into instant weariness. "Dad, I wasn't trying to talk her *into* anything. I only wanted. . . ."

"Well, she said she could stay at your place instead of at the hospital. And it was your idea."

"Okay, but I didn't talk her into it. She said she doesn't want to die in a hospital. I figure that's fair." My tone is belligerently defensive. We are even-steven on this one. "I told her I'd look after her if that's what she wants."

"Look," he disputes, "you can't give her half the care they give."

"I'm not so sure," I interject, my mouth tasting suddenly bitter. "Look how they've been treating her so far."

"They're doing all they can. More than what you can do."

"Sure. Writing her off as a complaining little old lady making a big deal over a dose of the flu. Telling her to come back Monday when the doctor is in. Then she is damned near dying and they don't know why. Come on, Dad." My every word is seasoned with disgust.

He clears his throat and moves one gear down into deeper bass. It's the ministerial bulldozer positioning itself to clear the deck. "Look. There's no way that you could handle an IV, or any of that stuff. Who's going to do injections at midnight? If there's an emergency what are you going to do? You'd be stuck up there on that mountain of yours. Useless. Like tits on a bull. Besides you've got the kids and Andreas to take care of."

"Andreas can take care of himself."

"You can't do it." We pause in silence for a few breaths. Time to reassemble our verbal forces. "Dad, what if she doesn't care about all that? What if she cares more about being with people who love her even if they are not so competent?"

"She'd *better* be cared for by people who are competent."

"What if she *wants* to be at my place, have home-cooked meals, be able to visit her grandchildren in a more relaxed way?"

"Well then, take her your bloody home-cooked meals but don't get so high and mighty that you think you can be cook, doctor, and nurse all rolled into one."

It is clear that my tone isn't helping this conversation any, and I know that diplomacy is more important than being right. Still, it's easier said than done to shift gears and step outside of our history of arguing with one another. I instinctively change track and run some logistics past him. He has the grace to hear me out. I have already checked out most of the details of home care so I know what help I can expect from the Red Cross, the Homemaker Service and the Public Health Unit. Gerry, the nurse at our doctor's office, has said that she could teach me how to do injections, and our doctor has agreed to be Mum's physician if she wishes. Mum likes and trusts him. I go over all the details of the support that is available, and make sure that at least Dad knows I am not being flip and unprepared. So far, so good. I am verbally surefooted.

Then I blow it entirely. I end my explanations with the most asinine comment imaginable, "Heck, Dad, our doctor said that if a junkie could learn how to shoot morphine that I could, too." How I can think that this would lighten the air, God only knows. I am struck with incredulity at how I can still do this, and wonder when on earth I will ever learn how to talk to my father. He isn't the only nerd in this conversation. I expect hot rage, but this one must appal him even worse than I can imagine. His answer is cold. "She needs more than the skills of a junkie to keep her safe and comfortable."

I should stop and apologize, but it doesn't even remotely occur to me. "Dad, Mum is not asking to be kept alive for ever. She knows that it's just a matter of time. . . . It's sort of like how things were with Vanessa. I didn't have to learn the whole four years of nursing school. All I needed to know was enough to take care of one person." There is a child-like whine to my voice that I can't shake loose.

"Look. When I was in a coma I sure as hell wouldn't have wanted some nincompoop like you trying to run the show. Not all doctors and nurses are saints, but they sure know a heck of a lot more than you ever will. They're ready for it. You're not. Plus they have millions of bucks worth of equipment and drugs. Your mother deserves the best."

"What if Mum decides that home care is best?"

"Well, you keep your bloody nose out of it. Besides, you put her up at your place and how the hell am I supposed to visit?" This one galls me because he hardly ever visited her even when she was in a nearby hospital. It seemed to be too much of a hassle for him. Still, I am not so dense that I can't hear his hurt, his need to make these decisions, his need to feel included.

"The boys said they'd take turns driving you out. You'd be able to see her just as much as you could in the hospital."

"Sure, and how the hell do I get up your stairs?" His voice sounds tired and sad as though the wind has been sucked out of his sails. His weakness softens me up.

"I'm sure Andreas could build a ramp." Throughout this conversation, Andreas has been sitting beside me, an axe blade dent of a furrow creasing his brow. At this last suggestion he relaxes, grins, and flexes his biceps, teasingly anticipating the strength of ramp needed. Dad weighs close to three hundred and fifty pounds; Andreas weighs about a hundred and thirty after a full meal and soaking wet. I smile at his antics and relax a little, feeling grateful for his presence.

"As if he needs more work," Dad observes.

"Dad, look, when you were sick, you wanted to be cared for in a hospital. If this were you, you would choose hospital. That's what you like. Maybe Mum feels differently. Anyway, it's up to her."

"You're as stubborn as your mother. I'm not going to argue with you any more. There's no way that she's doing anything but staying where she is."

The next time I visit Mum, she tells me that Dad has nixed the idea of any care but hospital care. She tells me not to worry just now because the doctors say she can go home in a few days. Everything will work out, she assures me. Her electrolytes are behaving themselves and she has been able to handle a fluid diet. Tonight she will try her first solids.

"I'll work on Dad changing his mind," she says. "You have to go at it slowly."

THE OFFER OF CARE

ও

Long before we got this far in Mum's medical crises, Andreas and I had decided that we wanted to be able to offer home care to our parents and to his special aunt, Tante Gertraut, should they ever need it and ask for it. While designing our circular tower, we considered the needs of a room that could be used to that end. We didn't know what it would entail, but we did try to make our home open to the possibility. We also had the resource of an uncommonly supportive group of local physicians.

One of them had cared enough to call me a few days after I had brought Vanessa home with her diagnosis of Delange Syndrome. He had suggested then that Vanessa and I drop down to touch base with him. I had told him that I couldn't. I still felt too raw to go public.

"Okay," he had replied, "I'll come up, probably this afternoon." It was that simple. That was the way these doctors practised medicine.

He began his visit at our home with standard doctor procedures: tapping Vanessa's chest, prodding her tummy, manipulating her hip joints. Then he sat down with us in the living room, and left his standard doctor approach behind.

"You know, when it comes to stuff like this," he had said, "medicine is bankrupt. All we can give you is a label, a name. We can't change genes; we hardly understand them. Infant stimulation programs are worthwhile, but that's about it from our side." He paused while we absorbed this. "The useful thing for you two . . . well, for all four of you, is to regard it as a spiritual problem. Trouble is that now you've got a medical label that stands in the way. You're in danger of looking at Vanessa and seeing Delange, not Vanessa."

We then talked about how we were already encountering that. When an article I had copied from a medical journal referred to lowered ears, we put the medical picture beside Vanessa to check whether her ears were actually lower than ours. Her ears couldn't simply be ears; they were symptoms. (Two years later the word "cancer" would result in a similar kind of blinkering over Mum's condition.)

The doctor listened to us for a while, then made a tentative suggestion. "Tools like the I Ching or astrology or anything like that may be flaky, but they are a freer language. Sometimes they're more humanly useful than the medical texts." He paused. "Have you thought of having an astrological chart done on Vanessa? At least it would be another way of looking at her, at her strengths and weaknesses. It might help free you from the Delange label."

We loved the idea. It felt liberating.

Andreas and the doctor then moved on to talk about the music that they enjoyed and whether Andreas would sing tenor in his Christmas choir. They sang a few lines together, then the doctor played piano—for Sabrina, he said—who had just woken up. For at least half an hour, he played a whole range of improvisations that spoke to all the feelings tamped down inside us. His music had a way with hesitation that made me think of Tuts Washington, but its essence wasn't New Orleans. It was right then, right there. It was cedar boughs and wood smoke; it was babies and feasting and grieving. He had the wisdom to play the silences as truly as he played the notes. This was the art, the healing, that the hospitals could never deliver.

THE COLOSTOMY

ć

23 June 1984

Three days ago Mum checked in to her local emergency ward with more abdominal pain and was ferried to St. Paul's Hospital by ambulance for emergency surgery. Once there, an emergency operation opened her up and cut away half her bowel, which did not prove to be cancerous but was, in the words of her internist, "riddled with holes like a colander." He was furious that it hadn't been caught before now. It was right there on the X-rays taken months ago. So much of Mum's pain could have been prevented. Heck, the whole colostomy might have been prevented. Did she need this? This internist knew Mum from years ago when she and Dad used to go to St. Mary's Kerrisdale church. Although Mum usually looked like many a garden-variety dowdy, elderly lady of limited means, he treated her in a manner that indicated that he held her in high regard.

When I visit, Mum is fibrillating in pain. She is beyond being angry at this turn of events. Since her potassium levels are low, she is having liquid potassium fed into her veins through an IV. She is in quiet tears.

"Don't let them do this to me again. This is the worst. . . . It's like molten metal poured straight into my veins. . . ." Her nails dig into the palm of my hand as she grips me fiercely,

"Sharon. . . . It burns. It burns!" This from a woman who has had gall bladder attacks and then her gall bladder removed, whose first child was born after forty-eight hours of hard labour, and who went on to have four more live births and one miscarriage. This from a woman who has gone through the sufferings of bladder cancer, and has had her bladder, uterus, and Lord knows what else cut out. This from a woman who knows the painful invasion of bone cancer and now the loss of half her bowel. My eyes fill. I am bankrupt for words.

On my drive home, the day is gloriously sunny, but its warmth and brilliance leaves me untouched. The muffler of my Rabbit has just detached itself from the manifold, and with each touch of the accelerator I sound like an adolescent male driver in heat. Drivers at each traffic light hurl scathing glances at me, but I don't care. This roaring suits me to a tee, better than the sunshine.

RESPITE

ę

I am more than ready for a holiday. The children are coming with us, and we are driving down to Ashland, Oregon. Andreas and I have tickets to six days of theatre. Luxury. The theatre provides babysitting too. For now, Mum's condition is stable. I can afford to flee. She and Dad are managing well enough with the homemakers' help. Mum has reduced her morphine and drives their car for local errands. Brian and Mikolt have our itinerary, phone numbers and dates, just in case.

We stop for a breather at our friend Doris's home in Seattle. Andreas naps with Vanessa so he'll be able to drive through the night while it is cooler and the girls can sleep. Sabrina has gone with Doris to take in the sights at the Space Needle. I savour my cup of coffee and am reading a book on historic notions of time when it dawns on me that what I really want to do more than anything else in the world is to go for a walk by myself. I stretch with the satisfaction of a cat, and delight in the fact that not only do I want to go for a walk, but I can. Only mothers of the very young can appreciate the extent of this luxury.

As I walk, I mull over names for our home. Andreas and I have been doing this for years now. We want our home to have a name, but we are lousy at naming things. Sabrina has named the entrance room to our house Ruskin, because Ruskin is a little town just before Mission, and this is a little room just before the living room. She has named the playroom beneath the kitchen Vancouver. It gives her a buzz when other children come over and she can say, "Let's go to Vancouver." They all paddle downstairs and feel terribly important.

The book which I have just been reading gives me an idea: Sabbath. I really like the seventh day set aside as a day of rest, a practice which started with the Babylonians. Apparently they discovered that camel caravans that paused to rest every seventh day met their destination earlier than those that simply ploughed right on through.

The initiation of a day of rest has personal meaning for Andreas and I. Two years ago, we quit working flat out every day, as had been our wont, and we rested on the seventh day. The first day that we did not work was eerie. It was as if someone had died in the basement and we were both avoiding coming to terms with the reality of a dead body. In fact resting was so alien to us that we kept catching each other cheating. I walk on, and smile just thinking about the sheepish look on Andreas's face, when I had followed the sound of a metal pellet being shaken inside a paint spray can. I found him in the basement touching up some scratches on his motorcycle fairing. It took us a month or so, but finally we learned how to relax, and just like the Babylonian camels, we covered more ground than before. I continue to walk, and try the words out loud: Sabbath Hill, Sabbath Bluff. Nothing quite grabs me.

I pass bungalow after bungalow with a car out front being vigorously soaped by the male inhabitant. It is Sunday. Three of them say "Hi" to me. This must be the United States, I think while smiling to myself.

As I walk, I remember a walk from a decade ago when I passed houses similar to the ones which I pass now. Back then the complacency of such houses offended me deeply. One by one I blew them up in my mind in slow motion. Then I got selective, and simply blew up televisions, fridges, stoves or sofas. After each explosion I played the film backwards in my head; the home, the fridge, the television, or the sofa would be reassembled, but changed. The juice which had spilled on the top of someone's crisper now lay separate on top of the glass, not welded to it as before. Into such spaces I imagined vitality. As I walked home, tall with pride, the houses and their inhabitants breathed deeper, fresher air. I had blown the status quo to smithereens.

It is curious. In the intervening years, I've grown to feel kindly toward these men who wash their cars, their hoses like umbilical connections to their unseen families. Even though I can't stand the military-style eagles on so many of these Seattle mailboxes, I no longer look down on the families who own them. As I pass their lawn-mowing and their neighbour-hood chat, and watch one man hammer on new siding, I feel delighted how at home these people are. Maybe the anger and arrogance that I had experienced on that earlier walk had something in common with the rages of my father, different only in their scale and their targets. Maybe the fact that I now feel so loved makes the difference.

Mum comes momentarily to mind, but for now the only thought I feel like following is the naming of our home. My mother's family home was called Mayfield, but then that was England. Canada demands something different in a name. Less settled, perhaps. Are there other words for Sabbath? At this rate, it will be years before I get it right.

THE PORTRAIT

ۓ

6 October 1984

Bless Mikolt. She has organized a family photo session. During the past three months Mum has been doing just fine, but in the past week or so she has started to sag. Until the past couple of days she has been doing all her own driving and shopping. How she gets Dad's wheelchair in and out of the trunk, I'll never know. Every time I try, the arms fall off and I darned near get a hernia. Early in July she weaned herself off her daytime morphine, and decided that aspirin did just fine for the cancer pains. She has taken her colostomy in stride, saying, "When you've got one bag, another doesn't make a great deal of difference." For a while the opening of the colostomy was painful enough that she would wince whenever she passed a stool, but after a while that pain abated. Recently she has had new abdominal pains but the internist figures that they are probably just adhesions from the surgery to repair her wrecked intestines. She's not so sure, but shrugs it off as part of the smorgasbord of pain that seems to be her lot these days.

Mikolt, who is paying for the studio time and one print each, has asked for sepia tone. Specifically, she doesn't want colour. The pictures will be expensive and she wants them to look classy in spite of the rag-tag look of our clan. Dad, of course, has secretly asked the photographer to do a series of shots in colour as well. I decide not to say anything in case it will make Mikolt look angry in the picture. Since she's carrying the ball here, I especially hope she and Brian and her kids look great. I never look that good in pictures, so I simply adopt a passive stance. At least that way I don't look silly.

Mum is dressed in a light yellow blouson dress with a green glass necklace for contrast. She is slimmer now than she has been for years but bears few outward traces of the incredible crises she has recently survived. Her hair has thinned, and is brushed simply to the side. Next week I have promised to take her out to buy the wig that she wants. Dad is wearing his usual shorts. Since he lost his leg, he refuses to wear long pants. He positions himself front and centre, and grumbles when the photographer seats two grandchildren in front of his prosthesis. The dress of my brothers ranges from Martin's other-worldly musician look to Struan's laid-back ruralese to Brian's classic blazer and tie. Andreas and Bruce represent the middle ground of fashion here. Quite a crew we are. I love the way we cover all bases. Mother tilts her chin defiantly and the camera flashes. Once, twice, five more flashes and we have it: not only our first family portrait ever, but also our last.

BARGAIN HARBOUR

ĉ

12 October 1984

Jan Elsted and I are on the first day of our four-day writing retreat at her mother-in-law's cabin at Bargain Harbour, near Madeira Park on the Sunshine Coast. It is a modest panabode, with more books than the copious shelving can truly handle. The walls and tables are filled with old Norman Rockwell calendars, pictures of cats, old family portraits, and enough dust and clutter for half a dozen households. This is not a space where the domestic arts are given high priority. The curtain hems are held in place with rusted clothes pegs.

To earn the right to be here without children I have made myself a solemn promise—secretly of course, since I would be embarrassed out of my skull to admit it—I plan to do a complete rewrite of the first six chapters of my parenting book. In other words, I will cram the better part of a month's work into four days. This expectation is decidedly ridiculous. It is also typical. The level of compulsiveness that Andreas and I share is both a well-worn joke, and a major concern to our friends. In the Schroeder–Brown household one must always be productive—no fools or triflers please! I do have to laugh at myself. Yet I have arrived with a wracking bronchial cough and have forgotten to pack any pens and pencils. Me, of all

people! I could suppose this is an accident, but then again, I did
remember my journal and a bottle of Scotch.

The pen which I'm using to write this with is Mrs.
Elsted's. It clots, leaving balls of fuzz on every third word or
so. The box containing my half-written parenting book lies
unopened by my feet. Ah, well. A pony of Scotch and a stare
out the window will be the ticket. I hold my pony glass at
arm's length and gaze through it to the drizzling calm of this
grey autumn day. The glass is slender and delicate, about four
inches high. It used to be considered an appropriate portion of
beer for a lady. It is cranberry coloured, an effect achieved by
minute amounts of gold mixed into the matrix that is melted
and blown into glass. It was my grandmother's.

Clearly I have OD'd on caring for people and need this
time for myself. Badly. After two years of waking several times
a night with Vanessa screaming for hours on end, with
worries for my mother heaped on top, I am feeling squeezed
by the vise of duty. Today I even forgot to kiss Sabrina
goodbye. As I drove out to the ferry, my desire intensified for
her goodbye kiss. I imagined the warmth and softness of her
lips on mine, and I ached for this imagined kiss to be real, for
the brush of her cheek.

A line from an old Dan Hicks and His Hot Licks song
springs to mind: "How can I miss you when you won't go
away?" Thank goodness, I weaned Vanessa this summer. My
tiny wrestling soul of a daughter. As I think of her, a nagging
voice in my head queries, "Was she ready to be weaned? Was
she? Was she? Was she?" I thought so. I think so. I hope so.
She turned two years old last month. She is eating and
digesting food much better. In some ways I could have breast
fed her forever, but in other ways, it made me feel so terribly
caged in, on top of everything else that is. If I hadn't weaned
her, I couldn't be here.

I swallow and savour the strength of my neat Scotch and
mull over the resentments that I need to resolve starting with

who gets what free time. That point of light at the end of the tunnel is so far off. Andreas gets child-free time because he needs it to write books, and his writing keeps us in groceries. The time that I am demanding is not so obviously productive. I may need it to stay alive, yet it always costs us, and the cost stands in the way of my taking it. Either we pay scarce dollars for a sitter, or Andreas pays with his time away from writing. I tongue the edge of the glass. Andreas needs to breathe, to be kept alive as much as I do. Maybe even more. His fears are larger.

I have Marguerite Yourcenar's *Fires* with me. I bought it after first reading excerpts when I was at Children's Hospital with Vanessa two years ago. I haven't read any of it since those first terrible months. Those excerpts which I read then, over and over again, like a secular equivalent of thumbed rosary beads, were deeply etched. I note my changed feelings as I read various lines:

> One reaches all the great events of life a virgin.
> I am afraid of not knowing how to deal with my
>   suffering.

> We say: mad with joy.
> We should say wise with grief.

> Wit? In grief? Why not, there is salt in tears.

Clearly my grieving over Vanessa's syndrome has taken me beyond fear of "knowing how to deal with my suffering." I feel tempered like good steel, perhaps even exquisite steel: unique, strong, durable and flexible. Yet just a moment ago, before reading from *Fires*, I felt diminished by resentments. I suspect that both views are true. I worry at this stage of my life how the shared commitment and familiarity between two people in a couple can not only sustain and comfort, but can also breed a life with days of no spark except that which is intentionally struck. The glorious accidents of grace are few and far between.

Not to be loved any more is to become invisible;
Now that you don't notice that I have a body.

I have a huge appetite these days to be nurtured by strokes of seeing hands, curious caresses of exploration, the flow of two bodies each into one. Ironically, I have needed this solitude to find my way back to desire. The cacophony in my head shouting out the needs of others has finally stilled. Andreas, I miss you.

13 October 1984

After a night of desirous dreaming of Andreas, I wake. The wood stove warmth has died down and I am in no rush to begin the day. In my mind's eye, I conjure the way Andreas's hair lies on the backs of his wrists, on his forearms and thighs. It would be so good to have some childfree time together. It is also one of life's ironies that the same two daughters who make that free time so hard to get also would make our free time together all the richer. After I have made coffee and set the fire, I wonder vaguely about how we are to live together in order to continue to be truly alive.

The heat from my coffee mug warms my hands. I absorb the slow rhythms, back and forth in the wide-armed wooden rocker. The blessed peace of Bargain Harbour. It's good, even necessary, to be here. Slowly, I savour my whole-wheat bread, made from the flour I grind at home, spread liberally with uncoloured, unsalted, unanythinged butter. Jan and I have hers-and-hers butters. Hers is salted.

Later in the morning, I break my armchair meanderings with an hour's long walk to Madeira Park, not that I got there. I probably took the wrong road; I ended up closer to Francis Peninsula. No matter. The point was the walk, although I also had the intention of a chocolate bar or three tucked into my head. A newspaper too. I always need a purpose, a goal, a level of keeping busy that stupidly satisfies me, mutt that I am. Jan is seated now in front of her old manual typewriter busily clack–clack-clacking. In my ease, I can enjoy her energy without feeling any need to match it. Heaven is time for reflection.

This morning before my walk, I opened the book on lesbians which my friend Ellen had given me as an early birthday gift. It was written by some friends of hers. "Their concerns are central to us," she had said with Ellen-style brusqueness, "whether you agree or not, and if you're not interested that's okay." I had recently read Ivan Illich's *Gender* and I was interested. I opened it in the middle to browse, and happened to start at a page about Ellen, her husband Reg and their daughter Valerie. I turned to the beginning and read the first sixty pages. When I went out for my walk I was still mulling over issues of gender.

Walking back from not getting to Madeira Park I reflected on how, at that moment of walking, I felt entirely "neuter." For much of my walk I had been unaware of my breasts, my belly and my arms; I had felt unconnected to the different womanly ways that my children and Andreas make me feel. My hiking boots had swung out rhythmically, ringing strong on the pavement with each step. I had walked straight from the hips, shoulders back, head held high, eyes alive. As I walked back toward the cabin, my sense of being "neuter" changed into that of being more fully "woman," being one with the earth. As I rounded the bay, I caught sight of a cormorant fishing, its fat body ploughing through the water, and I relived the birth of my babies. The brisk autumn chill on my thighs defined my sense of myself as a woman who was solid, sensual, maternal and invincible, a woman who had lived beyond youth. And this was good.

In these days of always being a "something" to two children, Andreas, the peace movement, and my mother and father, the feeling of being able to be nothing to anybody else, even just for a moment, was almost voluptuous. Not that I would want to stop there; all that I needed was a little taste. As I walked I thought of how much I enjoy purposeful action and thought, and yet at the same time how much I glory in my body of breasts, belly, arms, lips and skin. They are not really separate from action and thought, not for long.

Our language is poverty-stricken when it comes to finding words to describe how it feels to have a full breast tongued by a frantically hungry baby. Erotic is not it. The word is neither too much nor too little, just slightly sideways. As I continued to walk, my entire body smiled as I relived how my babies paddled my breasts with insistent percussion as they began to nurse. I felt their warm absent-minded strokes as their tummies filled and they drifted off to sleep, and that slight shock of cold when their lips parted and the spent nipple slipped free. Those days I felt at one with an ancient fertility figurine where the clay had been moulded into breasts and belly, the head, arms and legs long since broken off. Over time the statue had been reduced to essentials.

My mother's breasts are still beautiful at sixty-eight years of age. When she undressed at the cancer clinic last week, I saw the shoulders and arms that would be mine in thirty years; the bone underneath was delicate like mine. Her body has been thinned by her illness. It is at an in-between stage, neither sparse nor fleshy. Her breasts are still fuller than mine generally are. There is a soft line of flow from her neck down past the rill of collarbone, rounding out into a pucker of nipple, again not unlike my own. Her skin is crepier. There are no deep fissures of stretch marks but thousands of minute webbing lines of old-lady skin. She retains her own unique and particular beauty above the obscenity of her ileostomy and colostomy bags, and I wonder if my father or anyone else tells her of this beauty. I know that I never have.

MY THIRTY-NINTH

ℰ

8 November 1984

For all the sense of renewal that I feel today, last month's retreat to Bargain Harbour could have happened last year, or maybe to another person. Today is my birthday, and Andreas is waiting for me in the parking lot at the cancer clinic where I've been all day with Mum. He starts the car. I place my hand on his thigh, "No. Wait a sec, love. We're waiting for Martin. He's going to pick her up."

"So hasn't he done it? Where is she?"

"She's still inside. You can see her just to the left. She said I might as well go, but I want to wait till Martin gets here to be sure." My voice quavers. "It's been so bloody awful."

"What has?"

"What's that?" I point to the long white box in the back seat. When I am speedy I often focus on random objects that have nothing to do with the issues at hand. I grill Andreas on the specifications and cost of the ceiling fan in the box. We had agreed on buying this exact fan so there is no cause for debate, although I act as if there may be. We are already an hour later than planned and will have barely enough time to bolt down a meal. I take a deep breath and blow it out. "Christ! What a place. We've got to get rid of that bloody doctor. Mum's still in there waiting for Martin and I should be in there with her but I couldn't stand it any longer." I blurt out the last few words, still sitting rigidly and staring straight ahead and then burst into tears. Andreas holds back, looking at me with a mix of confusion, frustration and anger.

"Shit. I can't let her see me like this," I say. "Can you believe it? We went through the whole rigmarole. All those tests and garbage. Then Mr. Full of Himself Oncologist deigned to meet us. He poked Mum a couple of times. Asked her if she had any questions. She said, yes, she has a list. So he said okay, I'll be back in a minute. Then, poof! He never came back."

"What do you mean, he never came back? Didn't you have him paged or raise hell or something?"

"Of course I had him paged, Schroeder." What kind of a nit does he think I am? "Three times. Half an hour later the desk lady told me that he'd gone for the day. No point yelling at her. It wasn't her fault. Christ, what a bastard." By now Andreas has his arms around me and is comforting me.

"Jesus," he says, "what a prick."

I catch sight of Martin's car and pull myself together. I leap out and explain to him what has happened and where Mum is. He touches my shoulder. "Some birthday, kid. Happy Birthday."

Andreas and I go out for dinner, but nothing is right. My oyster hot pot tastes flat, and the shrimps in his dish can be counted on the fingers of one hand. Apparently the place has new owners since we were there last. Later, at the play that we had chosen weeks earlier, the dialogue flows past me in eddies as if I am a rock in the sea of audience. Dermott Hennelly comes onstage and I really try hard to stay focussed. I know Dermott somewhat. He's a good friend of George Payerle's. My friend Kinga once said he had the most luscious lips of any man alive. This notion lightens me up a little; for a while I follow each parting and closing of his lips. For now, that is all I am capable of. The dialogue of the play seems remote to me; the violation of my mother plays in the foreground of my mind. My mouth and stomach taste sour.

A CLAM IN A
HORSE RACE

ૂ

1 December 1984

The phone rings and it is Mum. Andreas has picked up his study phone and is listening in, which often happens. It saves explanations later.

"I have an appointment with a new doctor," she says.

"Great. How did you get his name?" I had asked local doctors to recommend a new oncologist after our experience three weeks ago but they'd come up dry.

"My doctor just switched me. It's pot luck, but we can't do worse. The appointment is at two o'clock on the sixth. I'll need you to pick me up at noon so we don't have to rush."

"Okay Mum, I'm clear, but I'll have to bring the kids."

As soon as we ring off, Andreas comes thumping down the steps from his study. "Why are you just capitulating to your mother's orders?"

"What orders? What do you mean?"

"She didn't just ask for a ride, she demanded it. What happened to all those cancer clinic volunteers? What about your brothers? Isn't it their turn?"

I am bowled over. It never occurred to me to do anything but what I just did. I glare at him, and don't even attempt to answer. He thumps back upstairs and I dissolve into tears.

Jesus. Jesus. Jesus! I am pissed off. I'll take her if I want to. What's eating him, anyway? As I peel potatoes, I work at calming down and seeing his side.

I've been driving to and from St. Paul's Hospital, the cancer clinic, or Pitt Meadows for eight months now. I know it costs time and money, and we aren't exactly flush these days. I put the potato peeler aside and vigorously blow my nose. Neither of us has been getting a good night's sleep. Last night Vanessa screamed for four hours straight, batting away at her face and banging her head. We're just too wiped. I can't remember when we last made love. Andreas needs to get away to write and to try on a full night's sleep for size. I need sleep, too. The house is a mess. I'm a mess. Shit! I blow my nose again. Mechanically, I put the spuds on the stove and start peeling carrots.

Andreas descends from his study with a softer tread. "Sorry, love. I don't know what got into me. It was just when I heard your mum ordering you around and I know how much sleep you got last night. It all seemed so unfair. Sorry."

We embrace like two wearied comrades in arms. Vanessa is sleeping right now so she'll probably be up till midnight. We both know this. Andreas's tenderness releases more of the tears that I had been trying to cap, but at heart I am comforted.

"I guess there's no one around to get mad at," he adds.

"I know. I know. Soon you'll have your time at Bargain. You need it. Maybe it will all feel better after that."

As I look past his shoulder my eye lights on our Pulp Press poster of two flappers sitting on their motorcycles, each smoking a cigarette, and the 1921 quote from Charlotte Perkins Gilman beneath: "Among the splendid activities of our age the nuclear family lingers on, inert and blind, like a clam in a horse race."

THE GOOD ONCOLOGIST

ε

6 December 1984

This morning, I am alarmed by a new look in Mum's face, a deeper terror than I have ever seen before. Her eyes are wild and don't rest on one spot. She has gotten a lot sicker over the last few days. Sheesh, I think bitterly, and she's still washing the old man's ass every day. When she goes for her coat she staggers badly, using the wall for support. My anger is too close to the surface for comfort. Mum doesn't need a scene, not today. I need to get out of here as quickly as possible.

"We've got to go, Dad. I've bribed the kids with store-bought cookies, but it won't last long." That's only partly true. I help Mum on with her coat, but when I offer her my arm she insists on staggering under her own steam with her cane in one hand, holding on to the wall with the other. She is spent by the time we get to the car thirty feet away. Instead of being able to seat herself smoothly, she controls a fall in the rough direction of the seat. Grimacing with every effort, she inches across the seat bit by bit, lifting first one foot into the car, and then the other. I know that it causes less pain if she can control all her movement herself. As she tries to slide up into a more normal sitting position, her coat slides down in the back and forces her shoulders down. I buckle her in. She looks like a human-sized rag doll stuffed into an oversize coat.

As usual she has her list. Before we drive off, she asks me to read it so I can think about anything else she should add. As I read, she repeatedly daubs lip salve on her cracked and scabbed lips. Her handwriting is shaky and uncertain, and words trail off into squiggles:

> pain still in knee thigh groin lower tummy right
>   back ribs
> little concentration
> slight sore throat
> lip sores
> blister on tongue
> drooling
> loss of appetite
> nausea
> very shaky
> bruising easily
> yellowish skin
> fluid on ankles
> constipation
> difficulty in swallowing
> sore kidneys

"This is some list, Mum. There's nothing for Christmas on there."

"Oh, you!" The wildness in her eyes is gone. We drive off talking about how all this feels, and how Dad is always after her to eat, eat, eat. Her mouth always feels parched and tastes awful, even if she is sucking a mint. By the time we get to the Mary Hill intersection, she is so acutely thirsty that we stop for a diet Sprite. She had a "cuppa" before we left, but it seems that she just can't drink enough.

"Is that on account of the morphine, Mum, or anything else that makes sense?"

"I don't know, dear," she says tiredly. "Maybe we should put that on the list. It's strange, with all that drinking you would think I'd be peeing lots, but I'm not. My urine is dark like tea—British tea, not your kind of tea —and it has a most peculiar odour." We haven't even got an educated layman's guess this time.

This is to be our first appointment with our new specialist. Tante Hanna, one of Andreas's aunts, has offered to help with minding the kids. We pick up Tante Hanna and arrive at the cancer clinic on time. After Mum's tests, we head two floors down for the two o'clock appointment. The receptionist is confused. No, they don't have a Mrs. Brown on the appointment sheet today, and the new oncologist is tied up in therapy.

Singed with exasperation at the cancer clinic, I show Mum's written confirmation. Thank goodness now for the record-of-visits card. The receptionist promises to see what she can do. I walk around the corner to tell Mum. Tante Hanna herds Vanessa away from the Christmas tree. Vanessa has already broken a bauble on the fourth floor. Tante Hanna may be a spry eighty-year-old, but a two-year-old still has the edge.

Mum looks near tears, so I offer her tea. "No, dear, just a cup of water." And we wait. After fifteen minutes, the receptionist comes around to tell us that she is sorry and that the mistake is all theirs. Two parallel booking systems are in the midst of change. The oncologist definitely wants to see Mum but he could be as much as an hour. Would we like to wait in one of the patient rooms where Mum could rest?

I wheel Mum in, and make her as comfortable as possible: take off her shoes, help her up to the bed, put a pillow under her knees, cover her with a blanket and turn down the lights. Now she does not resist any of my attempts to help. Thank God for Tante Hanna out there with the girls. I simply couldn't do this without her.

The oncologist arrives at about half past three, but as soon as we meet him, we both know that the wait has been worth it. He listens to Mum's every word, waits patiently while she reads from her list, then asks if she has more to add.

"Would you mind," he asks, "if I feel your spine to determine where that particular problem might be?" As he feels up and down her spine he asks where, exactly, her pain is. Does she feel it most sitting, standing or walking?

It is a treat having a doctor who takes Mum seriously and doesn't tell her simply to drink more fluids! Just feeling that she is being heard, that she may be right about the seriousness of some of her aches and pains, buoys her up enormously. I can see her spirits lift right then and there. In some ways it seems to matter more to her that she be considered right about her aches and pains than that their sum total may mean that death is closing in on her. The oncologist tucks her back in solicitously after his examination, and says gravely, "Betty, you're a very sick lady." Then he turns to me. "Would you like to come out and see her chart? Betty, is this all right with you, if I go over your chart with your daughter?"

I would have preferred that he do it with her there, but hindsight tells me that he was right. She wanted me to handle it and she really didn't want to know all the ins and outs. She was feeling awful, and she wanted to be taken care of.

Once we are out of the room and around the corner, there is no chart to be seen. Privacy for honest talk is obviously the purpose. The oncologist is simple, kind and direct. "Your mother's pain patterns indicate she may have cancer spreading up her back. I would like to do a series of X-rays to let us know where we stand. Then I would like to start a series of radiation treatments to help kill some of the nerves around the bone site in her pelvis to reduce her pain. She'd have to be in hospital for a week. The bed rest might help, too. She's a very sick lady. You should be prepared, this is likely her last Christmas." He pauses. "I'll go and see if there is a bed."

Five minutes later he is back with the news that there will be no beds open till Sunday. He is terribly sorry that he can't spare her one more trip back and forth to Vancouver.

"Okay, Mum, I'll drive you home now, then pick you up on Sunday."

With this Mum feels content, although by now she can't even stand unassisted. As I dress her, her gift for self-deprecatory humour returns. I wiggle her underwear up her legs and she jokes, "This reminds me of your Grandma Brown."

This is one of our old family tales. During Grandma Brown's last days, it was my job to dress her. One morning I had one heck of a time getting her large silk bloomers up over her bum and keeping them there. Finally, when I hooked them in one hand and was holding her up with her arms around my neck, she whispered in my ear: "Dearie, we'll not be making the burlesque theatre."

With Mum's arms around my neck, I ease her down into the wheelchair, and smile. "That's for sure. We'll definitely take a pass on the burlesque theatre."

On the drive home, Mum talks of preparations for the upcoming Christmas season. "I'm sure I'll be feeling ever so much better after the treatment. We'll go ahead with Christmas dinner like always. Father and I will do the turkey. . . ."

"Mum! Get real. I'll do the turkey. I can bring it all wrapped up so it'll still be hot."

"Well, if you insist. Then I'll do the carrot pudding and white sauce."

"Are you sure?"

"Of course. There's nothing to it. I'll enjoy seeing all my grandchildren again. I've got most of my Christmas shopping done. Maybe I can phone you to help with the rest."

"Sure, Mum. No problem."

The children are asleep in the back seat when we get to her home; I leave the engine running, hoping not to wake them. I go to help Mum out of the car, but she shrugs off my arm and walks to the house with more vigour than she had left it seven hours earlier. As I hang up her coat, she insists that I'd better not leave the girls out there too long alone. I insist that at least I'll make her tea before I go. I get as far as plugging in the kettle, and we declare a truce. She'll take it from there. Dad is glued to the television news.

I drive back into Vancouver. I've arranged to stay the week-end with George Payerle and Phyllis Surges. They've offered to look after the kids on Sunday so when I drive out to pick Mum up again, it'll spare the kids another drive. Andreas is up at Bargain Harbour writing with Crispin Elsted. The winter rain is heavy and slushy, and visibility is poor. As I drive I mull over the day. My happiness over Mum's improved spirits blackens when I think that tonight, and tomorrow night, and the next night, she will still be holding on to the walls to walk and yet will still be washing my father's backside.

KILLING CHICKENS

ह

9 December 1984

Before I pick up Mum in Pitt Meadows, I drive home to feed the cat and water the plants. I also drive by Ellen and Reg's to leave off some Mission for Peace documents. Ellen and Reg are out in the back yard killing chickens for the freezer. I watch attentively. The way that Reg kills chickens, I don't need to look away. In front of him is a stump with two nails sticking up an inch about two finger widths apart. He carries a chicken over and strokes its back while positioning its neck between the two nails. He talks quietly and gently to the chicken. "Take it easy, now." Reg's voice could calm anything. "This won't take long."

The chicken lies before me on the stump now, calm and motionless, while Reg holds its two feet between his fingers in his left hand. With his right hand he reaches down for the hatchet. His reach is deliberate if a bit jerky, a legacy from his stroke ten years ago when he was in his mid-sixties. A quick chop, and the chicken's head falls down while the decapitated body jerks and flutters. Still talking in a subdued voice, now to me, Reg steps over to some bushes, holding the body of the bird by its feet. Fudah-fudah-fudah is the sound of the wings as they beat randomly at the grass for some moments, then

73

are stilled. When the thrashing is complete, Reg releases the bird reverently and stands up to continue our chat.

One garbage can full of plucked carcasses overflows with cold water running continuously from the hose. Ellen plucks the second-to-last carcass and updates me on the activities of the Mission for Peace group. I had missed the potluck yesterday at which they folded cranes to decorate the Christmas trees downtown. Reg finishes wiping his hands. "I'll go get you a few cranes, shall I?"

"Can you spare three, Reg? I think Mum would like one to hang up at the hospital. She thought it was a great idea."

We had started making them after a survivor of Hiroshima had told us her personal story of that dreadful day, and of the devastation that followed. She told of Sadako, a young girl with leukemia who believed she could survive if she could only fold one thousand cranes, a symbol of hope in Japanese folklore. She died before she folded them all, but we fold them today to perpetuate her hope for peace. Reg hands me three cranes and the cards which Jan Elsted had printed on her own press: "This is our cry. This is our prayer: Peace in the World." It is the inscription at the Hiroshima Peace Park in memory of Sadako, aged ten. I tuck them in my windbreaker to keep them dry from the Scotch mist.

When I get to Mum and Dad's the Sunday afternoon television sports are on. Dad says hello, and then turns his full attention back to the tube. Mum's bag is packed but she is trying to remember just one more thing that she has forgotten. "Oh, well. It's no never any mind." Mum fusses. I bring her coat and help her on with it. She pulls a scarf out of her pocket to tie over her hair, and limps toward Dad. "I'm off, David." No response. "Well, I'll be going now. I'll see you in a week." My father proffers a fat shaven cheek for a kiss. Mum kisses him, pats his shoulder and leaves for the door. "I'll phone you when I get settled in. Your supper's on the sideboard." Dad salutes her parting with a goodbye gesture that has the air and the military crispness of a traffic policeman's signal. He doesn't turn around. I hold the door open for Mum. She comes toward me and hesitates momentarily. We exit into the drizzle.

THE FIRST NIGHT OF CRISIS

ع

11 December 1984

The full impact of Dad's message sinks in slowly. A resident doctor has just called him from the cancer clinic. Apparently Mum has a ruptured fistula. A foul brew of fecal and septic material has eaten its way out through her abdominal wall inflicting an open wound from the inside out. She has somewhere between a couple of hours and a couple of days before the septic process will claim her life.

"Geez. How did that happen? I just left her a few hours ago. She was okay then, a little fuzzy maybe, but hell, she's taking God's own amount of morphine." I stop to absorb this news. "What's the resident's name?"

I ask Dad to spell it and make a note so I will know who to ask for. Ever-practical Sharon here, on automatic pilot. "How 'bout I figure out what I'm going to do here and then I'll call you back? Do you want me to come and get you?"

"No. I'll come in the morning."

I am stunned. We had been readying ourselves for Mum's death, but this is all so sudden. After I hang up, I smack the table with my open palm, furious that Dad is choosing not to visit tonight. I am furious too that Mum is about to be robbed of the one thing she really wanted: not to die in a hospital. At very least she deserved that. My second reaction, after five minutes of pacing, is to know that I have to be there—immediately—and that I need Andreas. Phyllis and George quickly rally to offer child care for as long as I need it.

I call Andreas to update him. He doesn't question my need for him, but I feel compelled to assure him that I appreciate the gravity of what I am doing in asking him to give up precious writing time. I emphasize that we are talking hours or days here. I know he's just written seven chapters, in first draft, of a new novel in ten days. I also know how rarely that kind of magic strikes. But I need him—no one else—and I need him now.

Then I phone to tell Dad that I am going to stay with Mum. He tells me that Struan is on graveyard shift at the mill and Bruce and Martin are at band practice. As soon as Kinga arrives to be with their two kids, Brian and Mikolt will drive down to the hospital. They can pick me up.

I am trembling from head to toe. Phyllis volunteers to make tea. George offers a drink. I take him up on it. During major crises, alcohol is my drug of choice. Since none of us has had the time or energy for a liquor store run in the past few days, we are reduced to the dregs of some awful Cherry Marnier that I had brought along from Mission to use in a dessert. It is one of those liqueurs that I could never otherwise figure out what to do with. Drinking it now, straight, is about as satisfying as drinking Benylin. I regret my lack of foresight in not laying in a bottle of Scotch.

Phyllis tosses together a bag with mandarin oranges and some Christmas shortbreads made by her mum. She is being sensible. She tucks in some little glasses of grape juice, a bottle of decongestant, and another of expectorant to keep up the assault on my bronchial cold.

"Some of us after all," she jokes, "are supposed to survive the night."

We share a quick sideways hug. Geez I love that woman. I am still shaking when Mikolt comes to the door. It is snowing; otherwise I wouldn't even be here. I had wanted to drive home tonight. I had been diddling around in Vancouver long enough and it was time to get home. I was getting antsy, and ready to be back at work on my parenting book. Mum was supposedly basically okay, only in for treatment and tests. The cat needed feeding and the plants watering, but when the snow started falling the prospect of returning to Mission in the dark, then having to hike in the last quarter mile to our home with Sabrina and Vanessa and our gear, did not appeal. Thank goodness.

George and Phyllis's icy front stairs make walking in my shaking state more cause for shaking. By the time I get to the car I am quite giddy with shock. It isn't a feeling that I want to shake loose from. Part of it is an excitement that my looking-back, editing self will flinch from in embarrassment. But excitement it is. Here we are, the three of us on our way to something momentous. We are going to be out on precarious ground. The death of our mother. An orchestra starts up from the depths of my mind. How scary. How exciting. Will we really be up to it? The string section is gathering momentum. Real life, not your regular everyday numbing along. Fear. Grief. Terror. *Also* excitement. At the hospital, the doorman calls over to us at the elevator.

"Visiting hours are over at eight."

"Yes," I say, "But our mother isn't expected to live till visiting hours tomorrow."

The elevator doors close, we look smugly at one another, but I feel stupidly petty for my put-down of the doorman. To be sure, there were other ways he could have enquired about our presence, but that doesn't mean I couldn't have been kind. But that is part of the excitement: an arrogance that we are going up in the elevator for something important, and he isn't. That is the cut of it, as Mum would say.

We wave our way past the nursing station and sweep into Mum's ward, doff our coats and take up our stations. Immediately I feel calmer. Brian holds one of Mum's hands and I hold the other. Mikolt stands to Brian's left, the side to which Mum's head is turned. Mum's breathing is strong and regular. I had left her at four that day; a mere five hours later she doesn't seem that much different in appearance, but we put a whole different overlay of meaning on how she looks. From time to time we raise our eyes, meet each other's eyes directly, and then look down again at her. After a few minutes we start chatting in hushed tones. Soon Mum wakes up.

She sees Brian first in a start of amazement, blinks hard as if she can't believe it, and sinks back into the pillows. Then she turns her head slightly, blinks her eyes forcefully open in Mikolt's direction and looks quite pleased with herself as if she has indeed conjured up another person. She smiles as if to say "well, well" to herself and sinks back once again with her eyes closed, although only for a moment or two. She then tosses her head in my direction, I suppose turning to my voice, and blinks her eyes open again. Marvellous. A third apparition. In measured succession she blinks her eyes forcefully at various points around the end of her bed to see if she can conjure any more rabbits. To no avail.

On account of our laughter and sotto voce whispers, the lady behind the curtain in the next bed, a Mrs. Pickles, tut-tuts past us, waving her urine bag in front of herself as a symbol of reproach. After all, visiting hours are more than over. We can hear her lay down polite holy hell at the nursing station, and we burst into giggles. After a few moments of whispered consultation with the duty nurse and a little confusion—it is now staff changeover time—Mrs. Pickles is moved to another room. We have the whole two-bed room to ourselves with a freshly made bed should we need it. Since the patient names on the door still read "BROWN PICKLES," Brian and I revert to childhood humour.

During this night Mum's whole attitude, when she is conscious, is one of playful belligerence. When a nurse rinses out her mouth, she rouses herself on one elbow and demands with a tone of mock seriousness, "I want to know who ordered this," and turning aside to another nurse, "Are you in on this caper?"

She is like a child testing how far she can go with her elders. At one point when lack of consciousness swallows all but the first two words of a question that she is trying to ask, I rouse her to determine whether it is important to chase after the tag end of that lost question. She fixes me with a gaze that I can only describe as simultaneously penetrating and detached, closes her eyes as if to reassemble herself and then opens them briefly, and announces, "I'm doing a vanishing trick."

At some point my youngest brother Martin arrives, mumbling that he's figured he might as well come 'cause he wasn't gonna get much sleep anyhow, and you know, what the heck. Later, Brian and Mikolt leave because they want to let Kinga go home. It might be a long night.

For a while there are only Martin, Mum and I. It is a powerful night to share with a brother. We are bookends: youngest child and oldest child, now man and woman. We each hold one of our mother's hands and coach her to live, at least until Dad can arrive tomorrow. All colour has left her face, leaving her usually rosy cheeks an unsettling white, with even whiter striations that look as though they have been clawed into her cheeks and forehead. Whenever she startles awake, she instantly grins foolishly as if to reassure us. Periodically one of us lies down on the other bed, ostensibly to sleep, but we can't help but breathe our every breath in time with hers. After twenty minutes of shut-eye, enough to relieve the itchiness in our eyes, we return to the bedside watch, willing that Mum can keep the currents of her life's energy flowing. One more night.

Around two in the morning, my cousin Barbara arrives. I haven't seen her in years. She is trim, pert and immaculately dressed. It's not her fault, but her presence feels like an invasion; Martin and I had gotten so settled into our rhythm of caring. She cheerfully announces that she has brought food, and brandishes a box of Bugles. She takes off her coat and presses past Martin to take Mum's hand. "Betty, it's Barbara."

Mum opens her eyes and smiles a small acknowledgement before sinking back into sleep.

"Has anyone thought to read the Bible to her?" Barbara brightly inquires. This feels like the sudden slap of a wet fish across my face.

"No," I say, "we're just trying to help her rest through the night and keep enough energy so that Dad can see her in the morning."

The Bible is the last thing any of us needs. Martin and I are not Bible readers, and Mum's way of being a practising Christian has been in the realm of action, not words. Not that she didn't go to church every Sunday and carry her Anglican prayer book in her purse, but she never talked about it. Even though Martin and I scarcely know each other as adults, we had slid easily into the intuitive way of being with one another that comes only from sharing years of living together, from being of one blood. Still, as the night progresses and Barbara tells her story, I know how much my mother would want her to be here, and how wrong I was initially to resist her presence.

Over the years, Mum has been Barbara's confidant. We hear Barbara's stories in fits and starts through the night. She tells us that her husband has beaten her, and has threatened to kill her and the kids if she dares to leave him. Her oldest son, aged eight, has been receiving psychiatric counselling because he has been markedly suicidal. About six years ago, Barbara became a Jehovah's Witness. She is bound by their code, which amongst other things, demands total loyalty to her husband unless he violates their marriage in the biblical sense, by adultery. Once she hid from him for a few days until their pastor intervened. As I listen, my brain feels like a camera focussing in slow motion, taking in something that is too unimaginable to absorb.

I appreciate how much my mother's all-accepting ear has meant to Barbara and why she drove in from Richmond, despite some risk, to be with us. Even so, when Martin and I need silence, we take advantage of her willingness to fetch more coffee or to make toast in the patient kitchen down the hall. Then we return to being oldest daughter and youngest son each holding our mother's hand, each holding our thoughts, and—for the most part—each holding our tears.

This is the only night that we focus our energies on willing Mum to live. We all agree that if she doesn't make it through the night, then Dad's decision to leave off visiting until the morning will have been all wrong. It would be more failure for him to add to his already immense pile. Silently we squeeze her hands, willing her once more to go that extra mile for Dad. At times when her colour fades and her breathing stops for more than a half minute or so, we ask her to please take a breath. Please. She is exhausted with the effort. At four o'clock she asks the time, and how long until Dad will be there. At this point we are banking on him being there by nine. At six o'clock she asks again.

"After one more good sleep, Mum."

"You'll make it, Mum," says Martin as he punches her lightly on the shoulder like one good sportsman to another.

At half past five Barbara leaves for home. She has to get the kids off to school and then go to work herself as a sales clerk in a department store. If her husband is still asleep she isn't even going to let on that she has been gone. When she leaves, the three of us are left in a state of quiet and calm. The sky lightens, Mum sleeps and, after a couple of hours, Martin heads home. At eight, I buy a coffee and a *Globe and Mail*, brush my hair and teeth, and settle in for the day.

CONFUSIONS

* e*

12 December 1984

The hours tick past, messy with confusions. My brother Struan phones around eight. He isn't sure how he is going to get into Vancouver, because his van has broken down and he has lost his wallet. It must have slipped out of his pocket early yesterday evening while he was insulating the attic, and now it lies somewhere above him under one of many dozen batts of pink fibreglass insulation.

I suggest that he connect with Andreas who plans to be on the same ferry from Gibsons, and catch a ride that way. Then I find out that Andreas will be on a much later ferry. Too late for Struan to come in and get back home for his graveyard shift. I barely hang up when Struan phones back to say that he's dropping over to a neighbour's to sell one of his just-weaned piglets. Then he'll have enough cash to make the trip. He'll catch the next ferry. Martin, who went home a couple of hours ago, plans to sleep until noon and then pick up Struan at the Horseshoe Bay terminal. Regrettably, Martin oversleeps. By the time Martin drives over from North Vancouver and picks up Struan from Horseshoe Bay, Struan has only a couple of hours before he has to head home. The union contract will only give Struan time off *after* a family member dies.

At ten o'clock no one has arrived yet, and I am muttering

to myself. "Come on, you guys. We're in Day One of a possible two-day life span here. Let's get rolling." I phone everyone in turn. It is part of feeling alone and helpless; I do the only thing I know how to do. I act like the bossy older sister that I am; I'll get this show on the road, regardless. Unfortunately, all my phoning and fussing doesn't speed the slow unfurling of the day. Mum, fortunately, sleeps through it all.

Dad comes much later in the morning than we had expected. Brian explains later in a hush-hush corridor chat. Dad was paranoid about soiling his pants on the way in, so Brian had to hang around for an hour till Dad felt that his bathroom contributions were complete. Wonderful! Mum is dying and the whole world is still supposed to revolve around my father's bowels. Brian was none too thrilled about having to wash Dad's backside. Throughout the procedure, Dad complained about Mum not being there to do it. From Dad's perspective, everything is always "her fault."

While Mum and Dad visit, the rest of us retreat to the corridor. Brian and I indulge our disgust toward our father. As disgusting as Dad might be, we are just as disgusting ourselves. We pave right over any possible sympathy for our father's plight. Dad leaves within fifteen minutes; he wants to get home.

Finally, in dribs and drabs, the others arrive. First, Mikolt ushers in her daughters Ingrid and Korina, with Sabrina also in tow. All three of them have been scrubbed and brushed within an inch of their lives. Their hair is swept back from their faces with combinations of ribbons and braids. They look stunning, and quite British, like three little Pears soap girls. I hug Sabrina excitedly, grateful that Mikolt has attended to her appearance as well as she has to her own daughters'. Vanessa has stayed with George, which makes sense.

The girls are visibly nervous and tentative, backing up against the wall, keeping their distance from Mum at the end of the bed. It's not that they don't know hospitals; our family has had its share of that. Today, though, the children can sniff that this is different and are unsure about what to do next. While I mull over how to unwind us all a bit, Mum peers around her propped-up knees, looks quizzically at them, and says in a witch-croaky, Grimm's-fairy-tale voice, "They're nice enough girls, but it's too bad they're so ugly." The girls giggle with marked relief. "And too bad their parents raised them in dark caves, and beat them with big wooden clubs." Mum swings an imaginary club over her head and sticks her lower jaw out in mock ferociousness. "Argh huh!"

It is wonderful. We are all stripped of the overly serious demeanour of a death watch. Liberation! Thank you, Mum. The children move in closer, Sabrina sits on the end of the bed, and we laugh and joke about the indignities of hospital nighties, burps, and hiccups.

REVELATIONS

ટ

13 December 1984

At eleven o'clock in the eve-
ning, to my total surprise, my brother Bruce walks in. "I
thought it made sense to spend my birthday night here. Maybe
you can get a bit of shut-eye too."

I fetch him a beer which I keep under ice in a bedpan in
the bathroom. We toast his twenty-eighth birthday. "It's not
champagne, but what the heck, eh?" he says. It is so dry in the
hospital that nothing beats an illicit beer, especially when it
has been so artfully chilled.

"You know, at twenty-eight you're supposed to be em-
barking on a whole new beginning," I tell him. "Astrological
types say so, anyway. Life comes in sevens, and I forget why,
but the next set of sevens is supposed to be really significant.
Maybe you'll get to be a rock star." I tease him about his
musical aspirations.

"All right!" He grins. "Look at what Colleen gave me." He
pirouettes a few times in a new pair of skin-tight white pants.
He knows he looks great. Mum sleeps peacefully. "Martin gave
me a box of guitar picks. Perfect, eh? That's 'cause I'm always
scamming his."

As we savour our beer we chat about birthdays and the
cakes I used to make for him and Struan and Martin when

they were little. "Remember the turtle cake you made for Struan, and that friend of his who asked if he could eat 'the belly?' The whole goddamned belly?"

This is one of the unexpected pleasures of these days and nights here at the cancer clinic. In normal life I hardly ever see my brothers. We're all so different, yet now we feel so close. The sharing of our common memories warms us like the freshly raked embers of a winter fire. When we run out, our talk turns to Mum and we get practical.

"Come on, I'll show you the kitchen and where you can make yourself a cup of coffee." It's a dodge, but I can't bear talking about Mum's condition while we are in her presence, even if she is supposedly asleep. While I fear to hurt her by describing the realities of her condition when she can hear, I also wonder whether I may be hurting her just as much or more with our hushed hallway talks. I remember too acutely the effects of clumps of whitecoats huddled just outside the doorway when I was in Children's Hospital with Vanessa. *Whisper. Whisper. Whisper.* The flipping of their charts. Although I could sense major trouble, I couldn't sense what kind.

As Bruce and I amble down the hall we whisper sombrely. Bruce sings a short paraphrase of a popular tune, "Ah gotta know, what condition her condition is in." Then he asks apprehensively, "Do you think she's going to die tonight?"

"I don't know. She could, I guess. The nighttime is when she sags the most. It's really hard to tell. But look, wake me up if you get freaked, eh?" I know that Bruce and Martin don't feel as easy about being alone with her as I do. "Mostly she seems to need a whole lot of reassurance at night. The nurse will bring Ativan if she needs it, or a shot of Valium. The one who is on tonight is great to work with. I'll probably wake up anyway if things get out of hand."

It wasn't until a week later that I realized how likely it was that Mum's fear of death was heightened by a new-found fear of the dark. Once I hit on the idea of leaving all the lights on at night, she slept much better. As the old Bob Dylan song says, "They say the darkest hour is right before the dawn." I found that it is possible, somewhat, to cheat that darkest hour.

I show Bruce the resources of the patient kitchen, where there is coffee and bread, in case he gets hungry or thirsty. Sometimes, too, there are leftover untouched food trays available for people like us who are not part of the hospital's feeding plan. The night duty nurse drifts in and assures Bruce that he can call if he is unsure about anything. Once the kettle boils and I've brewed up an instant Sanka, we return to Mum's room and start talking about our kids and upcoming Christmas. Bruce is outrageously proud of Brookie, his one-year-old. He mimics how she does Greek dancing. We are whispering beside Mum's bed while he pirouettes. I imagine Brookie with her little baby fist behind her bum trying to snap her fingers before falling down. Mum stirs and we fall silent. Then he starts talking in serious hushed tones about Amanda, Colleen's child from a previous lover. Bruce has been with Colleen and Amanda since Amanda was a baby. In every way except genetically, he is her father.

"She was having trouble with school," he says, "but what the hell? Lots of kids don't get off on school. I wasn't that big on it myself as a kid, but you gotta get through, eh." He tells me that he and Colleen met with the teacher and talked about Amanda not paying attention and "assing around," and the next thing he knew he was being investigated for possible child abuse.

"What?" I say. "You've got to be kidding. On what basis? Just because she wasn't paying attention?"

Bruce explains the whole turn of events. When she was at school, eight-year-old Amanda apparently wriggled her bum around on her chair in a way that the teacher found sexually suggestive. The teacher reported this to the principal, who in turn called in the Human Resources Department.

"Christ! Vanessa rocks back and forth lots of times too.

Lots of kids do." I feel suddenly vulnerable. Sure, in Vanessa's case, we can point the finger at Delange Syndrome and its associated behaviours, but how would our family stand up to such scrutiny? I really don't know.

"The next thing I know is I come home from work early to find a social worker in my living room with these little dolls, saying to Amanda, 'Does your daddy ever touch you here?' I mean, Christ, I've taken care of her since she was a baby. What kind of a creep do they think I am anyway?"

"You mean you just came home from work, no notice, and there they are? What did you do?"

"Well, hell, I didn't know what to do. How should I know where all her squirming around comes from? Probably she's bored. I sure was when I was her age. Anyway, we go to see the social worker and the next thing we know they are telling us that they could make her a ward of the court."

"But how?" I ask. "Just because a kid squirms in school?"

Bruce goes into detail about the various meetings that were held and how all that felt. In the end, the only way to appease the powers that be was to have Amanda referred to a shrink for eight sessions. And if their family doctor hadn't made the referral, they would have had to pay for the shrink out of their own pockets, or else pay a lawyer to keep Amanda from being made a ward of the court. The outcome was that the shrink found nothing wrong with Amanda. He figured that it had to do with boredom, and that she would grow out of her "bad habit." Amanda still doesn't pay a whole lot of heed at school, Bruce explains, but he and Colleen are working on that. He talks proudly of Amanda's musical abilities. It galls him that even though his name was definitely cleared, he still has a record on the Human Resources files.

Amazing, the powers held over you when you don't fit the middle-class mould. Bruce in his black leather jacket, working as a plumber and rock musician, only recently legally married. Even his one-year-old baby wears a tiny black leather jacket. All that doesn't sit too comfortably with officialdom. As I listen to him spill his hurt over the whole thing, my anger at his dilemma roils. At the same time, I also imagine my friend Ellen's voice saying, "But just because he's your brother, how can you presume innocence? These things happen in *families*."

I am amazed that my own brother has been through all this. It's not surprising that I didn't know. We don't really know much about each other, Bruce and I. Hours later we talk ourselves dry and settle into the night together. He's brought a tape of Martin and him playing in their Young Pups band: he wants me to hear it, but it doesn't feel like the time or place for raw rock, even if it is his birthday night. I nestle into sleep, and Bruce pulls his chair over to the slice of light emanating from the hallway. He wants to write out some music on a couple of blank pages I've torn out of my diary for him to use. While I sleep he writes first a song and then a poem for Mum. When I wake, grateful and refreshed after four hours, he hands them to me.

"Here, have a look. I gotta take a piss."

The poem is a powerful and passionate poem of thanks. The last birthday present that Bruce has received on his twenty-eighth birthday is the gift of being able to reflect in a darkened room and to honour his mother.

ACTS OF GRACE

❦

15 December 1984

When Struan and his two youngest children, Conde and Iris, arrive just after three, Mikolt and I have been chatting in whispers for an hour or so. Mum is asleep. Later, Andreas drops in with Sabrina and Vanessa. Then Sabrina and Conde start playing tag, and everyone starts talking just that little bit louder to be heard over the ruckus. With the addition of four children under the age of six, Mum's room has been transformed into Grand Central Station.

Mikolt starts muttering into her knitting, "This is ridiculous. Simply ridiculous. Don't they have any respect for Mum?"

I shush Sabrina, not because Mum seems to mind the way the children are playing, but because Mikolt's certainty leaves me cowed. Awake now, my mother seems bemused. Andreas, alert to the dynamics in the room, corrals our two, hugs me and heads off. Struan is either oblivious or standing his ground. We talk for a while about the new sheep he is raising, a breed with especially long legs that puts on meat faster than his old breed. He points out that he forgot to take the bales of alfalfa out of the van before he drove here. That's why his kids are all bristling with straw. He glances at his watch.

91

"Holy shit! We've got to go if we're going to catch the ferry. Let's go, guys. Conde, say goodbye to Grandma." Conde obliges warmly. Then Struan snags young Iris, pulls a piece of straw from her hair, and holds her up to Mum for a goodbye kiss. Iris hesitates with a look of uncertainty that Struan can't see because he is standing behind her. Mum catches it quickly and blows Iris a kiss, offering instant absolution from the need to actually kiss Grandma. Iris's face lights up, and she blows her Grandma a kiss in return. First one, then another, then another. She clings to the rail on Mum's bed with the tenacity of a playful monkey. "That's enough, Iris. We've got to go."

Bless you, Mum. Another small rescue has been offered with grace. I savour the silence punctuated only by the clicking of Mikolt's needles.

At six o'clock I am sitting beside Mum's bed reading the newspaper, and she is propped up with her glasses on, peering intently at her section of the paper. She had asked for the family section. Everything would appear quite tickety-boo if it weren't for the fact that she is reading her section upside down. It leaves me feeling inexplicably happy. I glance over from time to time, and notice that a ladybug has landed on her bedclothes. Probably it hitched a ride with all the floral tributes. I find a bookmark for it to run onto, and then let it run off the bookmark onto the back of her hand. She holds her arm up and watches it scuttle down her wrist. She smiles up at me and customizes the traditional verse.

"Ladybug, ladybug, I'm flying away home. . . ."

After midnight I find myself reflecting that even though this may appear on the outside to be one of the hardest of times, it is also one of my most special. It has been years since I have had evenings clear to reflect on my life, my values, my loved ones. Somehow the nighttime is the most fertile time for writing and reflecting. During the daytime I fill much of my time reading ephemeral print. I start each morning with the *Globe and Mail*, and then move on to the *Province*. I even read the sports pages. Once I have digested both morning papers, I fill in the time with Rex Stout mysteries until the *Vancouver Sun* arrives. I lack the discipline for reflection during the daytime.

Mum is sleeping right now, but just half an hour ago I was awakened by the sounds of her quiet, empty retching. She was trying desperately to sit up, and with great effort was already up on one elbow. I leapt out of bed to help hold and support her and offer her the bedside bowl. Between retchings and before I had quite gotten to her bedside—all of six feet away—she looked at my feet and said, "For God's sake, child, get your slippers on."

As I held the bowl the most awful smelling brown clotted stuff came up. She may be in the middle of vomiting up the contents of her bowels, but she's still watching out that I take care of myself, still my mother.

KNITTING

ç

16 December 1984

I do a lot of walking here. The Cancer Hilton, as we jokingly call it, is small. There are thirty to forty occupied beds on this floor and another twenty or so unoccupied. This afternoon, many of the beds are empty as their occupants are downstairs undergoing the various treatments that the cancer specialists offer. When I walk the halls on evenings or weekends, usually bringing up another cup of real coffee to keep me going, I am followed by quietly beseeching eyes, the eyes of patients who seem to be hoping to change any passerby into a guest or a visitor who will stay with them. Some patients do ignore me and everyone else passing by; these people have their sights set solely within themselves. Still, I feel as though I wrong them all by passing them by. It's like passing the open guitar case of a street musician and not tossing in a coin. An opportunity for giving has passed.

At least half the women who visit are busy knitting. It makes me wonder what our generation of women will do, a generation less and less likely to be employed knitting sweater sets for their grandchildren. Mikolt is the obvious exception. For the older women, their knitting takes on the power of a sacrament. The quiet rhythm of their needles continuously creating garments of Sayelle yarn takes the burden of the visitor off the visited. One woman sits every day with her dying husband. The skill of her fingers tells me that she doesn't need to look at her work, but she never takes her eyes off it. It may be the only way that she can find the inwardness that she needs, and possibly that he needs too. I wonder how that little sweater will feel on the shoulders of the grandchild it's destined for.

My mother's knitting is here in a basket. She asked that my father bring it on what was supposedly the last day of her life. She had been knitting two sweaters for Christmas, one for Brooklyn, one for Vanessa, both of them knitted when she was deep into the fog of morphine. She had told me that she could only knit about a row at a time before nodding off. The stitches show it. There will be half a dozen so tight you wonder how they slipped off the needle, and then the tension slackens into softer and softer stitches, until you can tell that a new start has been made and the tension is tight once more. I've put the basket in the bathroom. I can't bear to see it any more. One night, recently, Mum woke up from a restless sleep to call out in an impassioned voice, "I hate knitting!"

Still she believes in keeping up and keeping on as much as possible. The part of her which is focussed upon living resolutely blocks out the part of her which is so clearly travelling toward death. She has made sure that Martin would bring in the Christmas presents which she had bought. She needs me to wrap them for her. As I sort through the pile of gifts, I can't find the presents intended for Ingrid and Korina. She remembers that she had planned to buy them each a diary. I tell her that I will do it for her.

"And Dad?" I ask.

"He really needs a sweater," she says. "Something washable, something that a homemaker can't wreck. Two XL should do it. That's what his windbreaker was. And beige, it will go with his burgundy polo shirt that looks so good."

"What about Brooklyn and Vanessa?" I ask.

"I'm knitting," Mum replies confidently. "I'm knitting them both sweaters. I have my wool here."

FEAR

ʔ

17 December 1984

It's two in the afternoon. Mum no longer knows where she is. She never has been able to remember how she actually got here. It's a total mystery to her, and she asks about it again and again. Just now she opens her eyes and announces, "I'm having trouble with geography."

"We're in Vancouver," I say, "in the cancer clinic."

"Yes." Her fingers repeatedly stroke the edge of the sheet as her mind fingers around the inadequacy of this answer.

"Canada," I say.

"Ah. Yes," she says as if it now all makes sense. This is not England.

"You live in Pitt Meadows."

"Yes."

Late in the evening Mum is thrashing around on her bed with a terrified look in her eyes.

"Phlegm. Thick phlegm," she says, tearing at her throat until it is red with raised welts. I sit her up and give her some ice cubes; her throat eases and her breathing settles down, but her body is still clenched. She stares rigidly into space, tight-jawed.

I tuck a few pillows behind her head, place a glass with

ice cubes in her hand and go back to half-heartedly watching the news on television. I glance over at her as she stares fixedly into space. Maybe if I ignore her she will be able to slide into sleep again. I am tired of having to be continually emotionally responsible.

We have been through this panic cycle a few times already today. I would like to say many times and be more worthy in my own eyes, but it probably hasn't been that often. I am feeling frustrated, inadequate and unsure of what the hell to do. Try as I might I can't shut her out, can't watch the news, so I come over once again and hold her hand.

"Is it really your throat, Mum, or are you scared about dying?"

"Yes," she croaks, and throws her arms around me in a desperate save-me embrace. We are a rocking tangle of arms and intravenous and nasogastric tubes. It is all so desperately wrong. At this moment I wish for a wisdom or magic equal to what she needs. I ache for a level of strength and vision that I don't possess. I feel bankrupt. Moments later, she falls back into bed exhausted with the effort of clinging to me.

"Hell, our family has a great tradition of dying in its sleep," I say, and mention Grandma Brown and Grannie Oddie.

"Quietly in their sleep," Mum says smiling softly. Soon her breathing eases up and she is asleep. My mind spins on to question whether this was really so: quietly in their sleep. There were no witnesses. They both died alone in their rooms, so we have always been free to presume quietly and in their sleep. I wonder, though.

When Mum wakes again, I hasten to assure her that my bed is only four feet away, and if she needs me at any time, day or night, I will be there. Her passage will not be undertaken alone. It is the least I can do.

After this first wave of assurances I start in again, more tentatively. "Mum, it feels to me as if you are thinking death will be like one massive wave that you will have to swim through whether you want to or not. That it will be like all the waves of pain, nausea and fear that you have experienced so far, but worse. And it'll come crashing down on your head and you'll be all alone."

She nods. "Yes."

"I feel like you don't know if you are up to it."

"Yes."

Maybe dying is like that, I think to myself. How can anyone know? Still, I talk to her about people who have "come back from the dead" with reports of music, peacefulness and a wonderful freedom from past pains; people who were able to float above the bodies they had just left to see those beneath and want to comfort them with the sense of release that they themselves were experiencing.

"Yes," she says. Her voice conveys appreciation for my efforts but not belief in my words. She smiles gratefully at me for my attempt. Finally she sleeps. I sit on my own bed and weep. If I didn't have two young children who need me, I really feel that I would risk a prison sentence to overdose her and put her out of her misery.

As I watch her sleep with the hated nasogastric tube down her nose and the intravenous in her right arm, it all feels so out of sync with the needs of the spirit.

Earlier today, I went out for lunch with Renate Shearer. We were co-workers at the YWCA almost ten years ago. We used to play early-morning tennis together, lousy tennis, not that it ever mattered. The whole idea had been our need for exercise and to vent our troubles, she with her estranged husband, I with the lover of those days. She is one of the true solid rocks in my life. Her warmth and understanding buoyed me up even more than the roast beef and Scotch, and they did so considerably. As I look over at Mum, I wonder what she would say or do.

At lunch, Renate told me that she and a friend have made a pact that if either of them gets into the state that Mum is in, the other will do whatever is needed to nudge death into its proper place. Renate's own mother died a painful death from cancer and she does not want to inflict that on her own children. I asserted that it didn't feel so awful taking care of my dying mother, that it felt natural and right.

Right now I don't agree with my own claim.

LADYBUGS

è

18 December 1984

It is early morning. I find a ladybug on its back on the window ledge, and gently drop it into the stiffest of the floral arrangements, the most funereal-looking one. Mum has outlasted you, ladybug. Rest in peace. You've flown away home. Lucky you.

This profusion of stilted floral arrangements is getting to me. Every day I toss another few chrysanthemums in the wastebasket, another piece of dried and curled holly. They seem to be arranged, in the florists' minds, to cover both bases: Christmas and death. I guess part of my anger about them is that it seems that Christmas is coming and death is hanging back. It is hard to admit how much I am counting on Mum dying. Soon.

As I pull another few dead flowers and toss them aside I feel irritated that no one seems to be coming by with new arrangements any more. I have to laugh at myself. Why would I want new ones when I can't stand the ones we have? I try to perk up what is left, combining two of them to make a decent show, but it's not entirely satisfactory. Even at the best of times, flower arranging is not my forte. Oh, well. I doubt that Mum would mind. At heart she's a kinder person than I am.

Some of the flowers have been dropped off in an out-reach of genuine compassion. Alex and Barbara Robertson brought the only arrangement that I like, a full bristle of pine offset with a red cloth ribbon and healthy flowers. I think that somehow they have the measure of Mum's condition. Barbara has had Hodgkin's Disease and knows a little of what being close to dying means. They are not like the people who drop off an arrangement at the desk. Those people really offend me. Are they so scared to come in? I pace back and forth by the window. Would it cost that much to say a word or two, perhaps to hold a hand for a moment? The ladies of this or that association offer their heartfelt wishes, sympathies and hopes for the best. . . . Shit! What do they mean by hopes for the best? Blatant hypocrisy. The spindly atrocity before me is like so many of them: a card on a plastic spike skewered into a square of floral sponge, with wired and crudely dyed carnations. Why don't I act on my convictions and throw it into the trash can? Mikolt would.

Mum has just woken up. Edna, my favourite nurse, a young woman who has just moved here from Newfoundland, drops off a pink gown for Mum. They look the nicest and there was only one left in the clean laundry stack. I tell Mum of Edna's kindness, but it doesn't register. At least today she knows that I am Sharon, her daughter. Yesterday I wasn't too sure that she did.

I go over to the window. The sun rising slowly from the shadows of the coastal mountains is a fine tonic on a clear morning like this. Someone had the wisdom to put the hospital beds on the top floors, with the best view. This morning I can even see Mount Baker and many of the mountains that I see from our home in Mission. A backwash of homesickness colours the picture: the smell of our cedar home, Andreas's voice on the phone last night. God, I miss him. I imagine Sabrina and Vanessa at home, still in their pyjamas. I remember that I promised to phone Dad at nine and it's ten past. Best go. He's a stickler for punctuality.

It is afternoon visiting time, and the resident doctor is visiting Mum. He stands about five foot two, even with the assist from his logger's boots. He is wearing a blue shirt and a carelessly knotted red tie. The vest under his oversized lab coat looks askew. I am curious to see if he has mismatched the buttons, but he hasn't. Its just that his body is off-centre. I guess him to be thirtyish working on being fiftyish. His manner is suitably ponderous.

A few nights ago Martin, secure with his six-foot-one frame had a good run at describing him. "Doctors, you know, always gotta look down. Just so you know how serious everything is and how right-on they're gonna be about it. Now that's a problem when you're just a tad over five feet. So you see, he kinda solves his predicament by fixing his gaze solidly on my lower button, then ducking his head sideways when he figures that he's gotta check me out to see if I'm still following him. Kinda makes him look like a bird drinking water, eh?"

We shared a good laugh. It feels good taking potshots at these guys. You can always pick out a doctor in the elevator by his look of goosed-up assurance. The resident speaks in such measured cadences it's as if he hasn't learned the verbal equivalent of proportional spacing. Today he slowly winds into his ritual, "How . . . are you . . . today . . . Mrs. Brown? Are you . . . in any . . . pain?"

Mum looks at him fiercely, and responds with her best upper-class, Cheltenham School English. "I want this tube out of my nose."

"How . . . is . . . your . . . nausea?"

"I want this tube out of my nose," she repeats with precise enunciation. I can't hold back my full-bellied laugh. Truly, I love her, love her persistence. After the resident completes his examination, he calls me out to the corridor for one of our hurried and almost furtive exchanges. If it weren't for his attire, one would think we were negotiating a dope sale, not sharing a medical prognosis. I wish we could talk in Mum's presence. He assures me that if she is still alive tomorrow, they will see if there is an alternative to a nasogastric tube. Several times a day, small amounts of blood percolate up this tube. It is irritating Mum's stomach lining.

After being comatose for most of the past day, Mum rallies when Tom Sampson brings Dad in late in the afternoon. Tom, now a police officer, is a native Indian whom Mum and Dad boarded when he came down from the Nass River for a year of off-reserve high school. Dad was the minister at St. Timothy's then, and my three youngest brothers were still at home. In the past decade, since Tom graduated from high school and moved on to college and independence, he has always kept in touch with my parents. Mum has always phoned to update me on his accomplishments with a note of maternal pride. Today she rallies to give Tom her best.

She actually tries and succeeds at conversation. She does this for Dad, too, and for the doctors, as if their presence signifies important time. Some of it seems to be the fruit of good breeding. She can seem so far gone, yet still modestly draw her nightie down over her knees whenever anyone but myself or a nurse comes in. I am grateful that the doctors still excuse themselves and ask permission before poking and prodding, even when she gives no indication of being fully conscious or able to respond. I am sure that some part of her still appreciates their gentlemanly conduct.

This is the first day since last Tuesday that I've felt she might be close to dying. This morning she was extremely agitated about not knowing who she was. As for myself, I am so thoroughly Anglo-Saxon that I took my grief away from her presence and had a good sob in the bathroom. Even so, I'm feeling strong underneath the tears. There is nothing more right that I can be doing with my life just now. My arms yearn to cradle both Sabrina and Vanessa, but I am doubly comforted that Andreas, in spending so much of his time and caring so well for them, cares also for me.

BEING THERE

ટ

19 December 1984

The events of last night really trashed me. Mum kept on trying to escape. She was determined to get two feet on the floor and stand up. She may have wanted even more than that, but even that was impossible, with an IV hooked up to an IVAC Impedence Controller, and a nasogastric tube hooked into a vacuum jar on the other side of her bed. I didn't know that she was still capable of such energy.

All day she had been mostly comatose, barely moving, yet frequently through the wee hours of the morning it was all I could do to restrain her. A couple of times I had to call for extra help as she tried to tear out the NG tube. She kept trying to fight her way past me in pure animal flight, fuelled by some primitive preconscious rage. An intramuscular shot of Valium followed an hour later by sublingual Ativan didn't touch it. A few hours later, when the gentle light of dawn started to backlight the outlines of the North Shore mountains, she sank into sleep.

A couple of nights ago, about three in the morning, she asked me once again to tell her how she had gotten here and what was happening. We had agreed that whenever she needed me to I would "tell the story" about her illness and why she was here instead of at home. Some part of her keeps putting her current realities on automatic erase. Some part of her cannot afford to know. After hearing once again the story of her admission and the doctor's assessment of her condition, she threw her arms around me, sobbing, "I'm not ready to die yet. I'm not ready to leave my children. And your father, how will he cope?"

A flurry of nurses bustles in and out of the ward beside ours. A woman is angry, alternately crying and yelling. As I lie in my bed listening, Jason's mother's face comes to mind. The white-gowned adults glide purposefully up and down the halls all night here just as they did two years ago during my stay at Children's Hospital. These are the people who are paid and valued. The mothers at Children's Hospital and the family members visiting here at the cancer clinic are treated kindly enough by the staff, but when we step over invisible professional lines we are gently but firmly reminded of our amateur status. Sometimes when I ask a medically pertinent question with the appropriate latinate phraseology, I catch a look in some doctors' eyes as if I am some sort of idiot savant, capable perhaps of playing Mozart but not quite able to write my own name.

Yet who does the healing around here? What can one fairly expect of paid staff? How can they be there to heal the pains that lurk underneath the clinically diagnosable signs? How could they ever have cradled Jason's mother so her baby could then have relied on her strength? Who is there to cradle the spirits of the hospital-bound men and women for whom death is just around the corner? The rage from the woman next door diminishes, probably the mixed blessing of the straitjacket of drugs. Again I feel we are right, I and the family members who make possible my presence here. Last night, Brian slipped me a couple of hundred dollars to cover our babysitting costs for Sabrina and Vanessa.

"You're doing it for all of us," he said.

Mum sleeps with the ragged breathing of the terminally

ill: many fast breaths close together, then a long pause inter-
rupted by a croaking gasp, then a course of fast shallow
breaths. I try to match her breath for breath just to see how it
feels. I give up after three minutes; there is not enough air. I
hope that I can hang on here. Even in the daytime when Mum
is most at ease, I have trouble leaving her. The doctors and
nurses intone the social work litany, "You need a break. You
must get out." Although they are right on some level, they are
also equally wrong.

When Mikolt or one of my brothers covers for me for a
few hours, I get out to shop for Christmas, but I am always
antsy by the end of my two-hour passes. I feel the wrenching
of the same kind of bond that felt so violated the first time I
left Sabrina when she was six weeks old. That time, I went to
see the Newfoundland theatre troupe Codco. They were hilari-
ous, but throughout the second half of their performance my
milk totally drenched my blouse and I ached for Sabrina. Now,
in much the same way, I am incomplete without my mother's
presence. After an hour away I start to feel that she is at risk.
I have to restrain myself from sprinting for the elevator up to
her floor. I am propelled by the feeling that "something might
happen," that she might want to let go, and that maybe she
wouldn't want to die without me being there, any more than
I myself would want to be absent.

BEING GONE

ح

20 December 1984

Today, the only response that anyone got from Mum was her succinct reply to her oncologist's question, "How are you?" She opened her eyes, looked at him somewhat disparagingly as if it should be obvious, and pronounced: "I'm a mess." Yesterday when he asked her the same question, she looked directly at him and said, "I'm here." That's the sum total. She's clearly had enough, although whether she's feeling any more at ease about dying, I don't know. It's not easy to figure out. Maybe her acceptance of death is like the tide, surging and retreating according to the fluctuating gravitational pull of her spirits. The morphine haze doesn't help any, but keeping her free of pain seems to be the least that we can do. A dial sets the rate on the IVAC; every day we turn it up a notch or two.

There's a new ladybug rooming in with us. Persistent little fellow, or maybe it's the same one in a fresh reincarnation. The way that death keeps on being cheated in this room I wouldn't doubt it. It keeps crawling up the window, getting a few feet up, and then half-falling, half-flying down again. Outside the snow is falling thicker and faster than I've ever seen in Vancouver. Mum told me once that it snowed like this when I was born. In the midst of that storm and after forty-eight hours of her hard labour, I was delivered into this world only a couple of blocks away from here. I was premature. My father described me as a purple plucked chicken clearing just over three pounds. Thinking of that makes me smile a trifle ruefully: some chicken. The snow is a good six inches deep with drifts a couple of feet high in the fire escape exits. I dig around in the floral arrangement where I had deposited the remains of the last dead ladybug. Its corpse is gone.

I walk down the hall to phone Dad, and end up having a rather extended conversation. Andreas had called me earlier to alert me; Dad had suggested to Andreas that he use his husbandly authority to call me off this whole business. The nerve! "And he thinks that would work?" Andreas had chortled. During the course of this phone call Dad keeps chiselling away at me: I should be home with Andreas, with the children. They need me more than Mum does, particularly Vanessa. Dad is digging hard.

I hold back my anger and explain how much it matters, not only to Mum and me, but to my brothers. Even though they are not in a position to care for Mum themselves, they are supporting me and so is Andreas. We have a long conversation, much of it a replay of our ongoing differences about how to best honour Mum's needs and wishes. For me there is no choice in the matter. I am a donkey plodding after the carrot. I have made a promise and I intend to keep it. Dad accuses me of heroics. We both score our points, but neither of us wins.

Halfway back along the corridor, I hear the unmistakable Lancashire call of my mother: "Help! Help!" Two nurses are ahead of me into the room. Mum stands shaking beside her bed with her arms half-raised and outstretched. "Help! Help!" Her NG tube is taut over one shoulder, and one arm is tangled in her IV and urine tubes. The three of us get her into bed easily.

"You were gone," she reprimands me. "I didn't know where to find you. I needed you." I hold her until she sleeps, then go over to my own bed and sob quietly, until I can find my way beyond my anger and my grief and fall asleep.

ALMIGHTY FATHER

ৎ

22 December 1984

Dad visited earlier today. It was his third visit since Mum was admitted on the ninth. I'm sitting here now with a tumbler full of neat Scotch to melt the fist I feel clenched in the back of my head, and I'm fuming. Mum's nose and around her eyes are still red with what I assume is her anger and sorrow, even though she seems to be sleeping now. I phone Brian and ask if Mikolt can come down and sit with Mum. I need to get out and walk or something. Brian goes one better and offers to take me out for supper. They'll be down in an hour.

I hadn't expected to get so completely decked. Bruce had wheeled Dad in about lunchtime, and the first thing Dad had done was to send Bruce and me out to fetch food for him. Unfortunately, by the time we came back with three shrimp sandwiches, the internist had examined Mum and gone. Dad said only as he bit into his sandwich, "Nothing new." I wished I had seen the internist myself. At the front desk the consensus seemed to be that there was no point doing any further diagnostic work. Mum was too near death. The doctor's report had described her as "moribund." It was a wait-and-see approach. Her oncologist, when he had checked in on Friday, wasn't expecting her to make it through till Monday. Still, I was cheesed off that the only action of significance today was action I had missed.

We had just finished eating when Mum's and Dad's parish priest dropped in, a little taken aback to see Dad with us. In the past, Dad had told me how Reverend Pike infuriated him by not acting on his suggestions for improving the parish. Reverend Pike nodded politely to Dad and myself, was introduced to Bruce, and then went over to Mum and said a few words to her. She stared blankly at him and made no response either of speech or movement.

"Can Betty hear me all right, Sharon?"

"Sure. She hears, and I'm sure she understands. I think the morphine just dulls out her ability to respond."

"Yes," Dad opined. "They always hear. That's the last thing to go in them." Dad spoke with emphasis on the "they" and "them." Reverend Pike's eyes met mine in a flash of aghast astonishment. Dad blithely went on to talk about how he knew about all this from his training at the Pastoral Institute. He then slowly examined his own fingernails in a theatrical gesture. Mum opened her eyes and turned her head to look at him, and tears welled up. I'm sure Dad didn't have an inkling of what he had just done. Reverend Pike just bowed his head and prayed, "Almighty and most merciful Father. . . ."

"Almighty and most merciful Father," I thought derisively, thinking of my own father. Good on the almighty but so much for the merciful. Does he even love her? I had always thought that behind all the day-to-day abuse he handed out there was a kind of love that we kids were simply not privy to, the tenderness of an Archie Bunker. Ten years ago when I had been visiting them up in Gibsons, I had browsed through some cards on the mantelpiece and seen her birthday card to him in which she had written: "and the secrets that we share," and I imagined an unknown passion. I thought of how we interpret our parents; I remembered listening to their lovemaking in the next bedroom when I was about eight years old, thinking they were having tickle fights just as Brian and I did. Now I can't imagine how I ever managed to invent something like passion for them. I can't yet forgive the sight of him proffering a fat sleekly shaven cheek for her to kiss as she left their home for good. Her eyes were wild with feelings—I ache, goodbye, I'm not coming back—and he didn't even turn to see her go.

ès

In many women's eyes, Brian is a gorgeous looking man. Once George Payerle, feeling both prescient and drunk, got offended at how pretty Brian was and butted a cigarette out on his cheek. In those days, George was known for being excessive. Still, tonight, I can see the eyes of many patrons at the Topanga Cafe are drawn to Brian. We order chicken tamales, refries and a side of tacos with hot sauce. We ease back to inhale our first beer. My finger traces down the sweat on the side of the glass. It is almost obscene how good I feel compared to an hour ago.

We dig right in to every contentious area of politics we can think of, and don't agree on a single topic. Brian worked on the campaign to get Vander Zalm elected mayor of Vancouver, while I am a card-carrying NDPer with my heart tilted toward the Green Party. The debate feels just fine. It's easy to tell that the couple at the next table are trying to figure out what kind of date we are. Brian and I argue passionately about school programs for English as a second language, about unemployment, about nuclear war. The puzzlement of the couple next to us amuses me. This is so much more fun than feeling caged in Ward 5.

When I get back from supper with Brian, I phone Struan to vent my anger over Dad's visit.

Struan disagrees with my interpretation. "You've got it all wrong," he says. "It's just that Dad hurt too much to show it. It is only in private that he can fall apart. You know the old man. He prattles on about his theological training because that is safe ground, a place where he can talk from without falling apart. He was King Shit there. What else has he got going for him?"

I hope that Struan is right, although my anger is still too pervasive for me to readily admit I could be wrong. I am still decidedly bullish. After forty years of constantly putting the needs of others before her own needs, this mother of ours deserves to reap her harvest from that love. Even so, when I walk back to the room I leave much of my anger behind. Struan is probably not all wrong either.

Our ladybug is now trying to scale the window. Last night it was at the head of Mum's bed. Every day I throw out more dead flowers, but we're still hanging in here: Mum, I and our ladybug. I settle into my bed. Enjoyment is not too strong a word for right now.

STOP THE STORY,
I WANT TO GET OFF

ؠ

4 April 1993

I need to step out of narrative for a moment to briefly discuss three issues that have plagued me in the latter stages of writing this book: privacy, interpretation and rage.

What right do I have, I have frequently asked myself, to invade my family's privacy and make this story public? Well, no right at all; I am not even sure that the issue falls into the question of rights, but rather into the area of responsibility. During the past decade, public thought has shifted course in a number of issues, family violence chief amongst them, specifically because many people have chosen to speak out and to oppose the restraints of family privacy.

There is a saying which goes back at least as far as the sixteenth century: "Charity and beating begin at home." Curious that the two should be yoked one to the other. It is also curious that our popular usage of this quote has shortened the phrase by deleting the reference to beating. Privacy does bring out the best and the worst in us. In writing this book, I have felt compelled not only to celebrate the best but to acknowledge the worst.

This process has not been comfortable. In the early drafts, my own rage toward my father was still too red-hot. I wrote hundreds of pages which I consigned to the wastebasket, and a few to a drawer for who knows what may come next.

I remember a dream from my early adolescence, one which I dreamed frequently in many versions. In it, my father was drunk and threatening. As his verbal violence escalated, I stepped between him and my mother. A struggle ensued, and he and I both fell down a long flight of stairs. I was unharmed and blameless. He was dead.

How much of this book is another version of that dream? I'm not sure that I am the best person to ask. All I can do is pay attention to how the freight of that dream has the potential to skew what I see. The fact that I hold the pen is an unfair advantage, of course, so as I have written I have tried not to forget that every event that I describe can be seen from as many perspectives as there are viewers. Mine is not the only, authoritative or final version; I do, however, have a responsibility to be true to the specifics as I saw them and to render them as accurately as I can. Only in that way can I hope that my words will transcend the limitations of my own perspective.

During the latter stages of editing this book my moral dilemma over violating my father's privacy became more acute primarily because of my own cowardice, which had expressed itself in a lack of clarity and a lack of resolve to be honest with him. Even though for several years after my mother's death my father was reasonably robust and healthy, I never gave him a manuscript of this book. I dodged responsibility on the basis that he knew that I had written it and knew that it contained some of our arguments, but had never asked to see it. I rationalized to myself that maybe it would never get published, and if it did, maybe the parts most likely to offend would be cut. It was just as possible, I reasoned, that he would die before it was published.

A year and a half ago, my father spent a couple of weeks

in intensive care fighting for his life. In the year that followed he lost half of his body weight, and almost all of his rage. During his regular Sunday phone calls he became genuinely solicitous. He regularly bought all of his grandchildren countless small but thoughtful gifts. In one year he spent more than two thousand dollars on books so that his grandchildren could have chances to read that his youngest children had been denied. Not only was he kind, he was also defenceless; he had dropped his shield of rage.

With hindsight, it makes sense to me that the intensity of Dad's rage peaked during the months that Mum was dying. Just as beating and charity are twin oxen in the yoke of privacy, so grief and rage are yoked together at times of profound loss. When Mum was dying, or just after Vanessa was born, I too experienced the connection. My own rage flared up unexpectedly and irrationally. Frequently its targets bore little or no relation to the source. I could get just as furious over an inappropriate flower arrangement as I could over the fact that the woman in the next room was dying alone. Mostly I needed release. A good explosion always cleared the deck and renewed my storehouse of energy. Again with hindsight, I understand why we were so often furious with doctors, the medical system and my father. In order to connect with our own sense of power, we had to challenge the powers which others held over us. We had to blow them out of the water.

Recently I came across a preliminary article on medical research that shed new light for me on the sources of some of my father's rage. The heading of the article caught my eye, "Those ugly body fats can create ugly disposition, study suggests." Apparently researchers at Edinburgh University have discovered that "men with raised levels of triglycerides— essential body fats—were more likely to be hostile and to have 'denigratory attitudes to others.'" The article also pointed out that raised blood triglyceride levels can be measured after eating a fatty meal, in people who have drunk a lot of alcohol, and in response to stressful experiences like accidents. I clipped the article and pasted it in my diary, and thought about it often. I imagined these triglycerides to be some kind of dinosaur of the blood, the kind that has tusks swooping out from between its eyes and a bony mass of defensive shield shadowing its shoulders.

Certainly the linking of stress, alcohol, fat and triglycerides could have had distinct effects on my father's behaviour. The loss of his leg and my mother's prolonged dying must surely rank high on the stress scale. Although I do not want to discount individual choices and responsibility, there are likely reasons why Dad became more gentle as his body winnowed down to half its former size. Some of these reasons probably lie outside the domain of medicine.

When I finally got up the nerve to tell my father more specifically about this book, he replied, "When other people hold up mirrors, you can't expect to like the reflection." He smiled and then adjusted his smile as if in response to seeing his image in a mirror, and then continued. "If anyone's halo benefits from a buffing in this story, it will likely be yours."

Dad adjusted his imaginary halo, and we both laughed. This is probably the man who was revered by so many for his skills as a minister. Maybe we just didn't know how to call forth that gift within the family, or maybe with too much history it was all impossible.

As we continued our lunch, I told him about the article on triglycerides, and asked him where he felt his own lifelong rages had originated from.

He paused briefly, and replied with an honesty that was both brave and disarming. "I guess that I just felt impotent. Also, I guess I was kind of angry at myself. I haven't made as much of my life as I could have." Too bad, I thought later, that raising five healthy children to become happy and productive adults doesn't seem to count for much in the male scheme of things.

Ursula Franklin, Canada's eminent physicist and peace activist defines violence as resourcelessness. I think of her often when I raise my voice in anger toward my children. Resourcelessness, yes, but there is something more. As a young adult, I called Dad's mix of moodiness, alcohol and temper "the Irish disease." That is what my Irish grandmother called it. These days such ethnic labelling is being lambasted, but even so, I suspect that genetic and cultural triggers were specific to my father's life and disposed him to act in the ways that he did. Perhaps what is just as important is that I recognize the heritage of similar triggers within myself, and celebrate that life has turned out as well as it has.

HEAVEN

ે

23 December 1984

I wake this morning at six to hear Mum singing the simplest of melodies. "Non nonon nonon nonon. . . ." It's the absent-minded kind of chanting that small children often do when they are playing in a sandbox. She sings the phrase, over and over again. For a few minutes I lie there, just enjoying it, then ask her if she would like some music. I often play Mozart or Haydn on the tape deck to help us through the night.

"Yes," she says. Then turning to me with a delightful easy look on her face she asks, "Are we music?"

"Yes. I am sure."

About fifteen minutes later, with a horn concerto in the background, she starts singing "Trés bon trés bon trés bon." Her face is radiant. I come over to sit beside her, feeling foolishly happy. We have become a brew of distilled happiness, separate from the trappings of the hospital. We rest several minutes with my cheek leaning on her shoulder.

Then suddenly she bursts forward into a sitting position, reaching up with her arms saying, "There! There! I see. . . ."

"Is it beautiful?" I ask, looking at her in absolute amazement. I have never in my life seen a face more compellingly radiant than my mother's in this instant. An earlier picture of her comes to mind, a picture of some thirty-nine years ago. She is gazing up at my father, unabashedly glowing with youthful vitality, obviously smitten, holding the bouquet of roses which he has just given her. Her casually tied white silk scarf lends an air of abandonment. She has just set foot for the first time on BC soil. The ten months of being a British war bride, waiting to emigrate and join her Canadian husband, are just behind her. The waiting train is in the background, its clouds of steam still lingering at their feet. I see this face now, with its mix of vitality, passion and devotion. Four decades have been shed.

She reaches with both arms and I support her from behind. I feel like a labour coach caught in the exhilaration of impending birth. She grabs hold of the IVAC pole to try and pull herself higher. I take both her hands and hold them up in the direction they seem to want to go, and am infused with a sense of overwhelming and total joy. This is beyond imagining. For me, it is beyond language. I am dumb. Time bends and arcs. We hold off breathing, and when we can do so no longer, she sinks back peacefully on her pillows, breathing easily.

I am spent with a mix of grief and joy, wishing with all my being that she could have died in that moment, could have been set free from her body of pain. In her sleep now, she is once again at peace, but her radiance has drained away. After half an hour, I am still lost in thought, still holding her hand.

CHRISTMAS EVE

è

24 December 1984

This morning I am busily wrapping Christmas presents. There are the ones that Dad brought the day he came with Tom Sampson, and the two or three little things I bought in Chinatown in lieu of Mum's unfinished sweaters and misplaced diaries. There is something for everyone now from Mum and Dad. Then there are the records I bought yesterday for Andreas. As I wrap them I relive the delight of yesterday morning. Mikolt had brought in her knitting and told me that I could have two hours off.

"Do whatever you like," she had said in her slightly Hungarian-flavoured English, implying an irony: what can anyone do in two hours? Mikolt is tremendous this way. A little shrug, and she will proceed to do exactly what is needed. For three days I lived off a casserole she brought in. As I cut a snippet of ribbon and tie a simple bow, I think of her attention to detail—my own wrapping looks comparatively humdrum; it lacks class—those extra little touches she is so good at. When she brings me in a home-cooked meal, she also brings in a cloth napkin and real cutlery. We have such different gifts, she and I.

Yesterday the slush was just melting on the side streets as I walked down from Broadway to Fourth. I enjoyed the walk in spite of my soggy feet. Maybe even because of them. The squishy sound as I walked underlined the fact that I was not in Ward 5. I picked up a cheese bagel to munch and arrived just as Black Swan Records opened. It was empty except for myself and the salesperson, so I asked her help in choosing some blues. It turned out she used to work for Co-op Radio; did she know her stuff! She pulled out half a dozen records by people whose work I had never heard of, and insisted on playing them for me. Of course I went overboard and bought more than I should have. Now, as I read their jacket covers and gaze at the pictures of the artists, I keep hoping that they will be just what Andreas wants but wouldn't think to buy for himself. Koko Taylor—God, she looks earthy—an ample exuberant black woman with a gold front tooth and a voice to match.

I bop around my bedside crooning improvised blues to myself in a raspy whisper, as I snip and tie along with the twelve-bar beats. In no time at all the wrapping is done, and I eye the pile with satisfaction. Mum's morning is peaceful and full of conversations that seem to parachute in from nowhere, that to most people would mean nothing. "Regrets," she says out of the blue.

"Regrets?" I look up from my wrapping. "What about?"

"Betty."

"That you were christened Betty, not Elizabeth?"

"Yes." That one I got lucky on. My middle name is Elizabeth because Mum has always figured she got short-changed in being christened Betty. I've liked Elizabeth well enough that we've passed it on to Vanessa for her middle name. Strange what snags us, the regrets that each generation nurtures against its parents. The morning goes like this: short wakeful periods with conversations blown in like one little fluff of dandelion seed after another.

I am packed and ready to go long before I expect Martin in to relieve me. I start listening for his footsteps an hour before he is due, realizing as I do it how hungry I am to hold my children, and to hold and be held by Andreas. Finally Martin arrives and helps me to pack the car. Mum is asleep when I leave. "Good luck, tiger," I punch Martin in the arm. He's embarrassed by hugs, at least I think he is. Or maybe I'm the one who gets embarrassed.

It is still light when I head up our road, but the dusk is advanced enough that the outside darkness frames and highlights the glow from the inside lights of our home. I leave everything in the car and race up the stairs. What a treat to open a door with a round handle! In institutions they open as you walk up to them. It feels as though I've almost forgotten how they work in real life. And Jesus, here we all are. Home at last. Hugs at last. Am I ready for this!

For a few minutes Vanessa holds back from me, staring. I swallow disappointment. Of course. She needs a little time. We collapse together on the chesterfield in a puppy pile, Vanessa sitting on Andreas's lap with eyes that absorb everything. Sabrina, Andreas and I are all talking at once, and most of it somehow gets heard. This is heaven. The press of all these bodies that I love so much, the smell of our home mingling the wood smoke and cedar which I can only smell after an absence. The tree is an eighteen-foot cedar cut out back, as yet only decorated up to the six-foot mark. Somehow it is perfect for this particular Christmas.

CHRISTMAS DAY

ૅ

25 December 1984

I am back with Mum again. I feel more at home here than I did at Andreas's father's where we spent this afternoon. We had Christmas ducks and all the ritual trappings of a Mennonite Christmas. Usually I love it. It's a counterpoint to the raucous Brown family approach.

Today I felt for the most part as though I was watching it all from the other side of a one-way window. Tante Hanna and Andreas's youngest sister, Chris, fretted and argued over whether the ducks were cooked just so. It was territorial kitchen stuff. No real harm in it. There is history there that neither of them can unravel. Andreas's other sister Angie and her husband Ron were late; Ron had gotten into an argument with Angie about her staying up half the night making marzipan. It's his ass-backwards way of caring. Every family seems to have its own versions. Today I just stood outside it all and watched like a Martian. Crazy. I am just as capable of such niggling myself. I too can go to pieces over curdled hollandaise or an underdone bird. This sharpness in the air shouldn't come as a surprise during the stress of Christmas preparations. I'm not sure why it all felt so foreign.

To all outward appearances I listened attentively to the German poems, prayers and Bible readings. In reality I soaked up the presence of my children. I absorbed the softest of sounds as I barely brushed my cheek against the downy fuzz of Sabrina's cheek. My chin rested lightly on Vanessa's head, cresting with her every breath as she leaned her back against me. The smell of the two of them, their warmth. I soaked it all up to take back to the cancer clinic. The rest of the family buzz and ritual washed past me. My time was up before the meal was served, so I took a plate with me to microwave in the patient's kitchen.

Bruce was taking care of Mum when I arrived. He had spelled Martin off in the morning, and was anxious to get back to help Colleen with the kids and their Christmas dinner. That was fine by me. After such a hermetic life here, I had found all the press of family a bit much.

It is dandelion fluff time again with Mum.

"Old friends," she pronounces.

"Thinking of old friends, Mum?"

"Yes."

"They're thinking of you too. Lesley Large and I don't know who all—Pat tells me half of England—have phoned her home asking for news of you and wanting to send their love."

A few moments later: "Elizabeth?"

"You mean Elizabeth in England?"

"No."

"Sharon Elizabeth, me?"

"Yes."

"I'm here."

"Can you help me sit up?"

"If you like, for a bit."

"But I don't have my shoes on."

"That's okay. You don't need your shoes on," I assure her.

"How do your friends sit up? Without their shoes on?"

I put my head on her shoulder, and she giggles. After a bit, she sleeps. It is already dark. I stare out the window at one of the windows in another building that always unsettles me at night. A backlit shape looks like someone about to jump. In daytime I presume the shape to be nothing more and nothing less than a huge paper Santa Claus. He's been on the verge of jumping for three weeks now.

Martin has just dropped in, and asked if we could walk in the hall. Mum is sleeping; I explain to her sleeping body that we'll just stretch our legs and be back in a few minutes. I never know if she hears me.

Martin is troubled about last night when he spelled me off. He felt that he had been totally unable to assure Mum that everything was okay. She was agitated that I had gone home, and that she had not gone with me. When Bruce relieved Martin at dawn, she had continued to question him over and over again. When was Sharon going to take her home? Struan is probably right that she is only alive now because she is determined not to die in a hospital, but it has been only recently that Dad has also accepted this. Part of Dad is angry that Mum is so bloody stubborn that she just won't die and be done with it. Why, he wonders, does she have to drag out her suffering? Yesterday he gave in. He will let her have her way; she can come home with me. I tell Martin the details that I have worked out with Andreas in preparation for her move to Mission. We agree to put the plan into action ASAP.

As we plan for Mum's future, it also seems as though she could die tonight, now that she's made it through to Christmas. Every night she has long bouts of chainstroke breathing. Her hands are curled in the manner of those on death's edge. Doctors knowingly observe these and similar signs, and say, "soon." It hits me that none of us bought her a gift for Christmas. Not even flowers.

This evening Andreas, Sabrina and Vanessa arrive unexpectedly. What a treat! I'm ready for my final Christmas gift of the day, just being with them. Andreas has brought a special Christmas Bunte Teller, a decorated basket filled with pfeffernusses, marzipan and other Mennonite delicacies. Angie, Chris and Tante Hanna have sent them. Sabrina has brought her violin and Andreas announces that she has a few pieces to play for Grandma. While I've been away, she has taught herself some Christmas carols.

Sabrina opens her case, methodically rosins and tightens her bow, then snugs the violin in under the softness of her still slightly baby chin. She darts a quick look over at Mum who is sleeping, and lays into a spirited version of "Joy to the World," followed by "Angels We Have Heard on High." By the second tune, the door is filled with nurses. Sabrina turns to the cluster at the door and plays on, revelling in the attention. "Hark the Herald Angels Sing." My eyes are filled with pride and joy. I gaze over at Mum who hasn't moved and appears to be asleep. Andreas has Vanessa in his arms; if I look at him now, I know I will burst into tears.

My pride is quiet. The nurses are more outgoing, exuberantly lavishing praise on Sabrina's performance. One of the young nurses quickly snaps off a few shots on an Instamatic. Another nurse kneels down by Sabrina, takes her hand, and asks if she will play for a few other patients.

I go down the hall with them to a sweet white-haired lady from Terrace, immobilized with spinal cancer. She smiles radiantly at Sabrina through her tears. Her hair is so white it shines like a crown. The gentleness of her wrinkles remind me of Grandma Brown at about the same age: late seventies, early eighties. Somehow in women who aren't too lean, their wrinkles get softer with age.

"Thank you, my sweetheart. Merry Christmas."

GOOD AS A JUNKIE

26 December 1984

We gather around Mum at mid-afternoon: Sharon the shift nurse, Sharon the ostomy nurse, and I. My last such coincidence of Sharons was in grade seven. The memory of those three Sharons evokes pictures from that time such as the day when I came home from school to find Mum seated inside the playpen reading a book. She was so pleased with her own ingenuity, of finding a way to be momentarily free of clinging, cuddling children. I shake my head to jar myself back into the present. The ostomy Sharon holds up a tube of paste. I must pay attention, though I am spinny with lack of sleep. My crash course in nursing is now starting in earnest. I have a lot to learn before I can bring Mum home, and I have two days to learn it.

Whatever has been happening inside Mum's diseased abdomen has put an end to any bowel activity. The colostomy opening for bowel movements a few weeks ago looked like a rose pink anus; now it is just a scab, as thin as new skin covering a burn. Sharon tapes fresh gauze over it. No problem. There won't be any care required here. Mum's urine system is also straightforward. Sharon rehearses the details for me, but nothing is new. She puts on a fresh disk and bag which should give me a few days at home without having to change it.

"Now, saving the worst for the last." Ostomy Sharon pries gently at the edge of the fistula disk. I move around to her side of the bed and place the backs of my fingers on the reddened flesh around it. It is surprisingly cool. She goes to wash her hands to keep the infection of one hole separate from the infection of another. The last time that I bagged Mum's fistula a week ago, she was conscious, and trying to see. She kept on telling me that I was being really quite silly since there were only two bags. Why was I doing a third? Even when she saw it, she denied its presence. She tried to poke her fingers in, so I had to bat her hands in order to get the job done. I can't cry about that now, though God knows I want to. "Focus, Sharon," I mutter silently to myself. "Focus. Focus. Focus."

The contents of this opening smell so vile that it makes my stomach want to crawl away on all fours. I'm getting used to it though. I'm learning how to steel myself against the worst of it. The worst time was that first night the fistula opened up. That night the gases from the wound were so acrid that my eyes smarted even though Brian, Mikolt and I stood in the corridor outside while the nurse attended to Mum. Today, when Mum hiccups, the acid flow comes faster than gauze and hands can move. It burns a border around the wound. There is nothing to do but curse inwardly, apologize outwardly, and daub as quickly as possible. The two Sharons agree that there is no solution.

The fistula opening is just above Mum's pubic bone; taping without catching pubic hairs is well nigh impossible. I don't ask why we haven't shaved her, and in retrospect it seems obvious that we should have. The bagging of her fistula has become more complicated over the past week. Necrotic tissue that looks like rotting umbilical cord is protruding. I ask if it is best to cut it off, or tuck it in. Is it living flesh? Will it hurt Mum if I cut it? None of us knows, so we cut it off because it makes bagging easier. Cutting it doesn't seem to hurt, though pulling on it does. The fistula opening has became larger, and a second fistula has eaten its way through a couple of centimetres above the first.

"Tell you what. How about if I do this one on my own," I offer. "Then you can see if I'm not doing it right." I stick the fresh tube of paste into my armpit while I remove the old disk and hardened paste. It's a trick Sharon taught me to warm and soften the tube's contents. I pave the hard red puckered flesh around the hole with new paste. Just as I get it perfect, the fistula fluids start flowing over the paste and into the crease of Mum's abdomen.

"Unfair," says Ostomy Sharon.

"Shit," I think to myself as I wipe it clean and start again. This time, I get the disk on before any more ooze starts. Congrats. Success.

We smile all round. Even Mum looks hugely pleased as if it was a good deal of her own doing. I pat her curled hand with relief.

"There, we've done it, Mum. No more messing around for a while as long as you behave yourself." Mum wrinkles her nose. Her patience through all of this has been amazing. Except for the occasional voiced grimace, she never complains. Believe me, I am grateful. If we are lucky this application will last for three days, but sometimes when Mum is turned to prevent bedsores, bags lose their seal, and the painful and tiring ordeal of removing old paste, and gluing on a new disk begins all over again.

I am settled down with my journal taking some late-night time to sort the jumble of terror and exhilaration from my day of learning.

I can actually do needles! I'm as good as any junkie on Main Street. I feel an overproof glow of self-satisfaction. Thank God for good teachers. Lydia, the nurse who had admitted Mum on our first day, is on duty this evening. She set my learning up in bite-sized chunks so I could master it at my own pace. She also didn't hover, for which I fervently bless her. A devout coward when it comes to needles, I was glad not to have an audience.

My first job was to measure the morphine accurately, then set up a dose in an IV bag. Lydia ran through the explanations of how many milligrams of morphine were in a cubic centimetre, and how many ccs were needed to make up a twenty-four-hour dosage. The morphine comes in 30-cc glass containers with latex tops. I had to turn them upside down, jab the needle through the lid, and suck out the entire contents of several containers. I took the last four ccs that I needed out of a glass ampoule, so I would know how to deal with them as well. The syringe that contained Mum's daily dose was as big as the syringes that vets use on cows. I recited the two important points like a mantra: keep everything sterile and make sure that there is no air in the syringe. It all sounded simple enough, but when Lydia left I inwardly panicked.

Just to settle myself, before I did anything, I ran through the whole drill in my head. Then I set up the syringe, needle, morphine, and IV bag just so. Still I was not quite ready to take the plunge. I did a dry run holding the syringe, but without unsheathing the needle. Then, when I felt confident, I took a few deep breaths and began, chanting the instructions in my head.

"Remove syringe cap. Insert needle into syringe. Click. Good. Alcohol swab over top of morphine bottle. Insert needle. Pull back on syringe. Take in a few ccs. Push plunger slightly. Expel any air. Tap syringe. Once more for safety's sake. Suck up remaining morphine. Again, till the little bottles are empty. Sheathe needle. Pick up ampoule. Snap off top. Unsheathe needle. Suck up the rest. Good, no air. Dosage complete. Sheathe needle. Alcohol-swab nipple on IV bag. Inject morphine. Done."

Somehow, after the first part, the task of attaching a harness to the IV bag and then setting it up on the IVAC was a snap. I am starting to feel like a pro. Still, I'd better get some sleep. There will be more kinds of injections to learn in a couple of hours.

Edna the Newfie is on. Great! At two-thirty in the morning we go into the dispensing room, where she watches me set up one needle with Valium and another with morphine. We head back. Mum is starting her night-time restlessness. I shake a little as I inject the morphine into the harness nipple near Mum's IV site. This is not the same as injecting morphine into a bag. This is going directly into my mother.

"Slow and easy." says Edna. "That's why we call it a slow push. You got all the time in the world. There. Hey! Wonderful." She gives me a hug. She feels like a kid sister. Later I have a cuppa to relax, but Mum is still restless.

Edna comes in, clucks and hovers. "Well, are you ready to take on an IM?" At my puzzled look she adds, "An intramuscular injection?"

"What the heck, eh?" We turn Mum onto her side and hoist up her nightie. Edna indicates the best spot, mid-cheek on Mum's bum.

"Now you remember just to tap it right in, eh? And do the pullback first, just to make sure you're not poking right into a vein. Then you shoot the works in nice and even like."

Inside I am shaking with emotional Parkinson's. Will I push too hard, or too softly? How tough is skin? What if her body is like butter and I go in too far and hit bone? Will I shake when I do the drawback? Will that hurt her even more? Well, damned if I am going to stand there like a fool with a needle in my hand. I imagine myself being Gerry, our own doctors' nurse, giving needles to the kids. Tap. Drawback. Plunge. Withdraw.

On the outside, I look for all the world like an old pro. Later, it takes an hour and a double Scotch to slow down my inner roller coaster and to find a few hours' sleep. As I dream I replay my new skills. In moments of partial wakefulness I review my own limits. As I sleep I regain the peace of knowing that although I am no expert, I am still good enough. I can believe that Mum will not suffer more because of my care.

I won't attempt to learn how to start an IV, just to revive one. Others will have to do this. There are lots of nurses here who can't get an IV started on my mother. Only one special nurse can thread her way into Mum's destroyed lifelines.

FEET ON THE GROUND

۶

27 December 1984

Last night the combined power of morphine, Ativan, and Valium let Mum sleep from three o'clock until daylight. Again, last night, it seemed entirely possible that any one of a night's worth of breaths would be her last. The pauses between her silence-shattering gasps were getting longer and longer. Around midnight she called out, "I'm coming through!"

During the next half hour, she was most concerned about getting to a wedding, although she was puzzled about whose wedding it was. She wondered, "Is it mine?"

All arrangements are being made for her to come home with me tomorrow. In her conscious moments, when she emerges from her coma-like sleep and the look of death slips away, she is incredibly excited. She frequently asks me to get her shoes. She thinks that we should go out for a bite to eat first. She has tried to climb out of bed a few times. I sit watching her as she sleeps and recall my last conversation with Grandma Brown, just hours before she died.

Grandma Brown stood five-foot-nothing, every inch of it Irish. I can still hear the cadence of her speech as she whispered her last words in my ear, "Dearie, you'll not be telling your father this now to be sure, but you and I must be

136

getting ourselves out for a drink. I know a place. It's down by the Burrard Street, don't you know, near onto Hastings or Granville or I don't quite know what, but we'll know it when we see it. I'll call you when they sleep. We'll have to watch the stairs, now. They're creaky, but they'll have to do. We can't be sliding down bedsheets *these* days. Pretend to sleep, dearie. I'll call you when it's right. Night-night."

If Grandma hadn't died, would she have actually tried to call for me when it was right? Or was my room just so far away that when she did call, I missed it? It never occurred to me at seventeen that I could have slept the night in her room. Do certain stages of dying impel us to get our shoes on, get out in the world, and get food or drink?

Once I brought Mum home, I realized how much she often just needed two feet on the floor. Nine times out of ten when she was fretful and unable to sleep, if she could just for a minute get the weight of her body supported with her own two feet, her agitation would vanish. As I would support her with a hug, I would feel her fretting fade away, and her tension dissolve. Perhaps in our dying there is some primeval need for flight that the mere act of standing can appease.

RELEASE

ﻉ

28 December 1984

My morning is spent racing back and forth from the fifth floor down to the first to use the phone in the social worker's office so I can tie up all the loose ends in Mission.

Mum is coming home with me today, as they say in the marriage ceremony, for better or for worse. Dad is quiet on this issue now. If we had been more sensitive to his needs, we might have arranged for him to visit her one more time at the cancer clinic. Rightly or wrongly, our focus is Mum. We have borrowed a hospital bed from the Mission hospital and a sheepskin from the Red Cross. Our local doctors have been alerted; I am to notify them when I get home. Meanwhile, it is snowing heavily in Mission. Andreas is frantically trying to keep our road passable, at the same time caring for the children.

"Don't futz around, love. The weather forecast looks like we're really going to be dumped on. The sooner you can get here the better. We'll get her up no matter what, even if we have to hire a D6 Cat. As it stands right now, we can still do it with a four-by-four." He continues with more details.

Some neighbours have already driven a four wheel drive loaded with gravel up and down our road several times to pack the snow down. Andreas has shoveled gravel on top of the snow to give traction in the steepest corners. Even so, no regular ambulance will be able to make it up our road. I phone the ambulance company to okay this. Our neighbour at the bottom of the hill works for the Dewdney Alouette Regional District Water Supply, and has offered their jeep to ferry Mum up the hill. If worse comes to worst, we'll carry her up.

"If it keeps up like this, we may even be looking at a helicopter." By now we are so bent on bringing Mum home that Andreas's suggestion of a helicopter, if need be, seems entirely reasonable. Notions of delaying on account of the weather don't even occur to us.

The head nurse, a tall bearded man who has lived for some years on Saturna Island, is familiar with alternative lifestyles. He has gone out of his way to bend the rules and make all this possible. The IVAC which wasn't supposed to leave the hospital is suddenly available. Thank goodness. I had phoned every medical supply place in town without luck. We had tried a gravity feed bag the night before, but the flow was uneven and therefore the dosage was uncertain. With the IVAC in hand I feel tremendously assured.

True to form, we have enough boxes, bags and stacks of stuff to give ten camels hernias. Sharon the duty nurse has loaded me up with half a dozen bags, all carefully labelled as to what the dosages for the different drugs are under different circumstances. She has also written brief notes about how to administer them: in the IV bag or as a slow push into the IV line. She has also noted for me the difference between subcutaneous and intramuscular injections. On the brown bag containing the valium, she has drawn a picture of a delightfully ample bum with a star on the left cheek to mark the desired injection site for an IM. This lady is thorough.

Finally, we have it all together. It's eleven o'clock. Not too bad. I am called over to the phone. It's the dreaded oncologist, the bastard who messed us up on my birthday. Today he is covering for the good oncologist, and I need to meet with him before he will sign the release papers. I cannot believe our misfortune. This turkey will never let us out of here.

We meet in the social worker's office. He starts by telling me that he doesn't approve. Mum's care is sufficiently complex that he doubts I can be up to it. I may share these doubts, but I sure as heck am not about to let on. He starts to grill me. What dosages under what circumstances? What method of administering the dosage? What will I do if the IV fails? Will I admit her to a local hospital if it all becomes a bit too much? (I lie, "Yes, of course. No problem.") And on and on. It has the pressure of a televised quiz show. One blooper and he'll knock me off the air.

Suddenly it's over. Grudgingly, without looking at me, he signs the release form and quits the office without comment. I don't know what to say. Alone in the elevator, with the door about to open for the fifth floor, I suddenly shut up. Without meaning to, I have been singing at the top of my lungs, "I am as corny as Kansas in August, high as a flag on the fourth of July. . . ."

When I get to our room, the ambulance attendants are waiting in the hallway. Together we transfer Mum onto the stretcher. There's nothing of her. She is so gaunt. With the white towel wrapped turban-like around her head to keep out the cold and the grey blanket tucked under her chin, she looks like a funereal sarcophagus. She has been given an extra slow push of morphine to endure the trip, and her eyes loll senselessly in their sockets. It is hard to imagine that she will survive the trip. My elation damps down. Brian has arrived to help packhorse the whole load downstairs. Sharon quickly strips the bed and bundles up the foam egg-crate mattress for us. She checks all the drawers and behind doors. She finds one last item: Mum's cane. I give it a Charlie Chaplin twirl.

This is my first time in an ambulance and I am fascinated. Mum's stretcher is latched to the wall and floor; the IV hangs from a hook in the ceiling. The IVAC is too tall, so we take it apart and lie it on the floor. We are ready to roll when Sharon the duty nurse calls me out to quickly brief me on what to do should Mum die on the way. "If someone dies mid-trip the ambulance crew must try to resuscitate, but you don't have to go along with that as long as you are prepared to take responsibility. Then they'll just head for the nearest hospital. You okay?" We embrace, then I climb back in, a little shaky from mixed excitement and fear.

I lean forward to squeeze Mum's hand. She squeezes back. "We're off."

The ambulance attendant delegates the "taking of vitals" to me. Every fifteen minutes I call out Mum's pulse, breathing rate and approximate temperature. At the same time I keep consulting the second hand on my watch to assure myself that the IV is dripping at the requisite twenty drops per minute. At Abbotsford, I ask the driver to pull over so I can give Mum a relaxant. It might help on the bumpy ride up our road; the lead time for it to be effective is about right. The dosage administered has to be recorded in triplicate for posterity. More forms! Between Abbotsford and Mission, the IV slows down to a third of its rate. I try all the tricks that I know to no avail: I stretch the harness, I check for kinks, I flick at various junctures with my finger, I loosen the gauze and then tighten it back. Still no go. I resign myself to the fact that we will need to ask one of the doctors to come up right away to get it going again. Not a great start.

At the base of our mountain is a gaggle of men, trucks and shovels. The fresh snow is about six inches deep; the boughs of the cedar trees droop under its weight. Andreas has put chains on our truck which is packed full with the hospital bed and related gear. We quickly decide that Mum will go in the water district's jeep. Andreas will take all the bags and boxes and each vehicle will take one ambulance man up front; they have to come with us to sign—what else?—more forms. Mum's stretcher fits in the jeep with an inch to spare when the tailgate is slammed up. I sit on the tailgate, holding her IV bag aloft, silly with fear and bravado. We snail our way up through gravel-speckled snow. One corner and we are fine, another, and the last one, and over the last hump. We've done it!

We drive right into the back yard and stop near the door to the room Sabrina has named Vancouver. The door is narrow. The ambulance attendants have to tilt the stretcher to make it into the room.

"We've done it, Mum!" I cry as I hover over her, still holding the useless IV bag high in the air. Mum opens her eyes, and smiles. Her fingers slide out from underneath the blanket and flash V for Victory. Andreas organizes the guys to help him load in the hospital bed. They grunt and groan as they stagger past us. It must weigh a ton. Then we are alone: Andreas, Mum and I. I gaze down at Mum with Andreas embracing me from behind. Mum's eyes are closed and her breathing is steady. I turn to embrace Andreas and burst out laughing. All the while I have been standing there, I have still been holding that useless IV bag above my head.

LATE AFTERNOON

੧

28 December 1984

"Look at the snowflakes, Mum, fat and big as corn flakes," says Sabrina. I smile; now I am the Mum. Playfully, I draw the curtains, making a little tent around her as she breathes fog circles onto the glass. Then I turn my back to her to check out how I have the room set up so far.

Vancouver is a circular, ground level room at the base of our four-storey tower. The kitchen is just above. Usually this is the children's playroom or a rudimentary guest room. The head of Mum's bed is beside me, between two windows on the south wall. Various bags of drugs, needles and ostomy gear are already stashed in the curving bookshelf above her head. To her right, under one of the windows, is a shell-backed easy chair, much worn and with shot springs. Its distressed upholstery is camouflaged by an old floral sheet. To the left are two chests full of sewing remnants, good ideas that I have never completed.

I have set up a mattress on the floor for myself. It is at right angles to the foot of mother's bed. The staircase up to the kitchen is at its foot. At its head are both the exit to the outside entrance and the bathroom. Our bathroom is actually more reminiscent of a ship's head than a residential bathroom; it is three feet wide, six feet long, and tucked underneath the kitchen stairs. The toilet is raised like a throne so it is high enough for adequate drainage to the septic tank. I have set Mum's disinfectant and talc on the back of the wash basin.

This is all makeshift but the shabby furnishings are somewhat redeemed by the walls which are clad chest-high in cedar. I wonder what I can add to make the room homier for Mum. I unpack the sepia picture of our family from last October and place it on a sewing chest.

As Mum sleeps on, I wonder how long her morphine will last. The IVAC is still leaning in pieces by the back door. I set it up by her bed, so we'll be ready when one of our local doctors gets here. He has promised to hike up after he has finished his patient rounds at the hospital. As I lay out the papers that I think may be of use to him, I glance at Mum's admission and discharge summary.

"This unfortunate 68-year-old lady was admitted for reassessment of metastatic, well to moderately differentiated carcinoma of the bladder." It pleases me that they describe her as a lady before they leap into clinical descriptions. The text then describes her episodic sweats, progressive weakness, loss of recent memory and her "pelvic tumour with inflammation, necrosis, and supra-infection."

The next page is so chock full of jargon that I hardly know what they are talking about. Thank goodness for the shards of Greek and Latin I can still resurrect from twenty years ago. I enjoy the challenge of puzzling various words from their root meanings. Then I balk, not on account of the language itself but because of what is being implied.

"On day of discharge, the patient's clinical condition was the best it had been over the two and a half week hospitalization." Like heck it was. She was at her best in the first week, not the last. What is this? The last paragraph states that she could "suddenly deteriorate and die, but it is also possible that she may linger on in a steady state, or, in fact improve." Are they covering all bases?

"Like heck she will," I think. I look at her for confirmation and am startled to see that her colour is much better than it was this morning. She is breathing normally, too; but she also did that sometimes at the hospital. I turn back to the report, holding firm to my own appraisal of her condition. It ends by calling Mum "an extraordinary woman." Well, at least that part is true. I decide that my own assessment—that she was only resisting dying because she was in a hospital—is accurate. We will keep her here for a few days. I am warmed by the thought that I'll be able to keep the promise I made to her last summer.

By the time the doctor arrives, true to his word, Mum is conscious and looking perkier than she has been since the start of this whole debacle. Since her IV failed on the way home she hasn't had any morphine, which probably explains her alert state. Without the constant morphine, though, why is there no pain? I had been so conscientious in insisting that the dosages be kept high in the hospital.

In an almost courtly manner, my mother thanks him for coming. After cordial introductions he sits down beside her and goes to work. He attempts to tap into her veins for close to half an hour, then stands up and flicks the IV needle into the wastebasket. His mouth is tight with disgust.

"This kind of needle is so fine that we use it on the skulls of newborn babies. Even with that I can't get a start."

I am appalled. Now we've done it.

"You'll have to manage your mother's pain by injection. I wouldn't give her as much as she had in the hospital."

I stare blankly at Mum.

"Tell you what," he adds. "Would you like me to do the first set of injections? Here, pass me the morphine. I've got a syringe handy in my stuff."

Even with this reduced intake, each dosage will have to

take two injections. It is too much fluid for Mum's body to absorb at any one site. I tell him that I'll be okay. I have enough syringes and needles.

As the doctor leaves, we joke that the IVAC pole is likely the latest height of fashion in coat racks: the high-tech industrial look.

A CUPPA

ॽ

29 December 1984

I wake with a start. Shit! It is 2:30 a.m., and I have overslept. This makes it four and a half hours since Mum's last injection. So much for the three or four hours I had intended. I bolt to the bathroom for a fast pee. Mum is still asleep. Hope I haven't blown it. It takes more drugs to stop pain once it has a hold. How could I have missed pulling the pin at the back of the alarm clock? Ah, well, too late to get all of a feather now. That's a Mum expression for you, I think, feeling better as I realize it.

My skin is electric with energy. Partly I have that heightened sense that comes from being precipitously awake when the body would be more naturally asleep. Partly it is also the terrifying uncertainty about whether or not I am equal to all of this. Once I have the first syringe filled, though, I am calm and able to absorb the peace of our slumbering household. Why is it, I muse while filling the second syringe, that the quality of peace in a sleeping household is deeper than in one that is merely empty? Mum awakens, and I give her the two injections. It goes much better than I had feared. I set my alarm, climb back into bed and am instantly asleep.

Mum sleeps peaceably until I wake her at six-thirty for her next two needles, and then falls back to doze. For whatever reason, she had no night terrors last night, and I wake feeling more refreshed than I have in weeks. Sabrina climbs into bed with me. We cuddle and giggle quietly while, overhead, we can hear Andreas making cream of wheat.

When I am up and dressed, and sorting out the next batch of needles, Mum props herself up on one elbow and asks if she might have a cup of tea. When I tell her, "Of course," she brightens immediately and hastens to add: "And I would like to get out of this blessed bed and drink it right there." She points to the old overstuffed armchair by her bed.

I am elated. I regard this as a new stage, oblivious to the fact that had there been an armchair by her bed in the hospital, there might have been times when she would have chosen it. This is all going so splendidly well that I don't stop to question where we are headed.

Andreas puts the kettle on. Neither of us is a tea drinker but I find some Tetley's Tips tucked away in the back of a cupboard. That will guarantee a potent brew! Mum prefers her tea British style, righteously strong, with a shot of milk to tone it down. None of this foppish herbal stuff. In a moment of inspiration I serve it in her Wedgewood wedding china, which she gave me a few years ago. The design reflects the gay abandon of the early 1920s. A riotously bright band of fruit chases around the brim, contained by a fine border of white and black squares. When I was eight years old I tripped and broke one cup from the set while serving her Mother's Day breakfast in bed. Now I place the cup and saucer reverently on the tray beside the warming tea pot. The perfect choice, as long as I don't trip again!

While the tea is brewing, I prepare to sit Mum up. Since she hasn't been out of a bed for three weeks now, I am not at all sure how easy it will be to get her into the armchair. Slowly I roll up the head of the bed as high as it will go, then tuck a couple of pillows behind her back. Now she is in an almost upright sitting position. Andreas hovers at the end of the bed in case I need a hand. I slowly lower her legs, one at a time, over the side of the bed where the urine bag is hooked up. Then slowly, ever so gently, with my arms under hers and my hands circling her back, I lift her up toward me, wondering as I do it if her cancerous hip and leg can stand the pain of motion, wondering even if her hip could break in its weakened state. With her arms around my neck, I support her full weight while she does a little hopping pirouette that turns her around, ready to sit in the chair. Nothing has come unglued. The pain hasn't been too much. It has worked!

I tuck her in, and Andreas presents her with her tea. Her eyes are flashing. She says nothing, but holds the cup with both hands wrapped securely around it, then hesitates with the brim barely touching her lips. She pauses, breathes in the steam for a moment, savours its warmth and smell, and extends her lips for a first tentative sip. "Marvellous," she affirms. "This *is* simply marvellous." Over and over again. Andreas and I stand opposite her and embrace one another. It *is* marvellous.

When another family doctor arrives to restart Mum's IV and check her out—having run up the hill, not walked it—we are feeling tentatively confident. Mum is pretty much in charge of herself. After the usual preliminaries of introductions, pulse-taking and stethoscope-listening she announces out of the blue, "I don't want that IV again."

"Betty, you don't need the IV," the doctor agrees. "Obviously, if you can have your pain managed by Sharon giving you injections, and if you can drink fluids and keep them down, then you don't need an IV." He goes on to point out to her that while she is doing so well, it is a good time to talk about how she would like to be cared for when things became less easy. Mum's response is succinct. I have never heard her speak with such assertion about her own needs. "When I can drink, I want to be given drink. When I can eat, I will eat. But I don't want to be bullied. If I say I can't, then I can't. And I don't want that IV again." She points theatrically toward the IVAC.

It's a great response. She does not want me to overdose her, but if she is ready to die, she wants to be left to the will of her own body. When she can eat or drink no more, we must respect that. Considering her condition during the past two and a half weeks, though, I am taken aback that she can be so articulate and to the point.

As the doctor puts on his boots by the front door, we exchange thoughts on where to go from here. I offer that I'd like to try reducing Mum's morphine if it can be done without increasing her pain. Getting down to one needle every three hours would be great.

"No problem," he says. "You've got enough common sense. Just take it down a bit each day. She's managed the drop from the hospital dosage just fine. You know, it could even be that her joy at being here is shrinking her tumours. It's happened before. The spirit is a marvellous drug." He puts on his red checked jacket, stuffs his stethoscope in the pocket, and gives me a gentle sodden hug. "You'll do okay. Give us a holler if you need anything. One of us will be up in a few days, sooner if you need us."

By noon the snow is three feet deep outside, and a bitter wind is gathering fury. Then the power goes off. All of Mission is out; it's not just our line. Three hours later when there is still no power, Andreas hikes down the mountain to pick up a kerosene heater from the Elsteds. We can still heat the house with our combination wood and oil furnace, but without the fans blowing the heat around, this ground level room gets virtually no heat. I find a white wool tuque for Mum and tuck a down sleeping bag in around her.

"Hypothermia. That's all we need now," I mutter, using black humour to keep my rising bleakness at bay.

While Andreas is out getting the kerosene heater, I am kept busy between keeping an eye on Mum, attending to the wood fires in the furnace and the living room fireplace, and caring for the children. Suddenly, as I am upstairs changing Vanessa's diaper, I hear Mum calling, "Help! Help!"

I race downstairs to find her on her knees on the floor beside her bed. Her urine and fistula bags have both been ripped off by the fall, and the carpet is soaked with urine and necrotic sludge.

"Oh, Mother. . . ." I mutter in disgust, more to myself than to anyone else, as I put my arms around her to pick her up.

"Where were you?" she asks. "I just wanted to find where you were." She lifts her head from my shoulder to glance at the expression on my face, and adds quickly and petulantly, "Don't get mad at me."

"Oh, Mum . . . I'm not mad. At least not at you. It's just a hell of a mess. I'm tired." Sabrina and Vanessa watch wide-eyed as I ease her over to the armchair. Vanessa, still bare from the waist down, walks over to inspect the mess on the carpet, and nearly steps in it. I yank her back abruptly. It is all I can do not to start sobbing. "Come on, you guys. Out of here. Mum, you stay put until I get a diaper on Vanessa."

I know that Mum can't budge out of the chair, so I'm safe. She hides her eyes behind her hands as if it is a game. I, on the other hand, must now get Vanessa diapered, deal with the carpet, change Mum's bed linens, wash her all off, then apply new discs and bags.

An hour later, Andreas troops in with the kerosene heater lashed to a backpack and a bag of groceries grasped in each arm. He can't see a thing. His glasses have fogged up with the inside warmth, and his beard is dripping with melting snow. His shoulders are sodden with wet flakes. I take the groceries from him and set them down, and ease off the backpack. As he polishes his glasses on his shirttails, he regales me with the adventure of sledding the truck down our mountain road. I can tell that he needed to get out and feel manfully useful. The physical recharge of a hike up the mountain has replenished his spirits. In comparison, my tales feel less than victorious.

Unfortunately, once we unpack everything, we can't get the kerosene heater to light. This sucks the wind from our sails. Andreas is muttering about wicks and settings, and I am offering all sorts of what-ifs and maybes when Mum peers over at us and chirps: "It doesn't matter. I'm just toasty fine, thank you."

We look up from the disassembled heater like a couple of startled gophers, and then turn to shrug to each other. Well, okay then. Since this is what we are stuck with, there isn't much more we can do. We hope the power will be on soon. Andreas reassembles the kerosene heater so he can better take it apart in his workshop. Whether we end up using it or not, he's determined to figure out what is wrong with the wretched thing.

"Tell you what, love. I'll get some laths and weather-stripping and nail that sucker good and airtight." He nods toward the back door, his hands full of heater, wrenches and screwdrivers. Good old practical Schroeder. He is back in a couple of minutes to secure the back door, then staple-gun a blanket at the base of the stairs to conserve heat. After he leaves, I tackle the carpet one more time to see if I can get rid of the grey splotch left from this afternoon's escapade. As I scrub, I hear a hammer pounding on the other side of the outside door. Must be laths being nailed on from the outside too. Andreas is making doubly sure.

I gaze out the window. The natural afternoon light has long since faded, and it triggers a memory for me. "Remember, Mum, when I was confirmed in that church in Metz, France, and there was a power failure when the bishop put his hand on my head, and I had to find my way back in the dark?"

"Yes, and you never learned, did you," she quips.

I laugh, and since I don't know what to make of that, I collect my gauzes, cloths and lotions and head up to make supper.

OIL AND WATER

ٷ

30 December 1984

This morning when I wake up it is bitterly cold. Mum is still sleeping so I seek out Andreas to find out why we have no heat, and whether he knows about it yet. He's already down in the basement removing wood from the furnace. His arms fling the wood aside with fury.

"We've got no oil. No fucking oil. I've got to start the bloody wood with kindling and hope like hell it works. Jesus fucking Christ."

"But I don't understand. We had both tanks all filled last September and we haven't used that much oil."

"Well maybe we have. Besides, I only filled one tank. Figured that's all we'd need, but look for yourself, there's no bloody oil." Andreas bends over to suck the disassembled oil nipple one more time, then straightens, spits on the floor, and tosses the line dispiritedly against the wall. There's no way I can help, and we have lived together long enough for me to know that he would rather stew alone. I go back upstairs to grind coffee beans. As I climb the basement stairs, my legs feel sodden with despair. At least I'll have a cup of coffee in peace and quiet, and see what happens next. Mum and the kids are still sleeping.

Half an hour later a cold, wet and bedraggled Schroeder slumps into a kitchen chair. "We're not out of oil. I went and banged on the tanks. One of them is still full. The bloody line is frozen, and it's not just the line. I stuck a lath down inside the tank. The stuff inside has turned to jelly 'cause it's so ass-freezing cold."

"So what do they do in the prairies? Put in methyl hydrate or something?"

"Yeah, trouble is who the hell do I call at seven on a Sunday morning to find out what to add and how much?" He stomps off, only to reappear fifteen minutes later. He has roused Bill Gordon, the Shell distributor, who has told him what to do. It will take a lot of work. As well, there are some supplies which we will need which we don't have on hand. Also, the fuel filter may be shot.

I'm starting to feel as though the fates are conspiring against us. The temperature has plummeted to twenty below. It never gets that cold here. Never. We aren't set up for it. Fortunately the power came on last night. Andreas digs an old clunker of a heater out of the basement for Mum's room, so at least she will be fine. The he splits up a block of wood into smaller pieces than usual, and shaves off some kindling. The fire in the furnace catches, and holds.

"Now we can't let that sucker go out," he lectures me, as he sometimes does when he feels himself under siege. It's frustrating to be on the receiving end, but I do tend to forget such things when my attention is divided.

Two hours later, while Andreas is still outside trying to free up the fuel lines, a neighbour calls. He has been out at his barn which is close to our well at the base of the mountain. "There's a huge geyser of water spurting out of your well. Looks like something's cracked. Matter of fact, it's been going for some time."

"You've got to be kidding," I say. "We've still got water."

"You maybe still got water, but you also got about a

fifteen-foot-high frozen fountain. Any minute now you probably won't have water."

A pipe has cracked in the cold, it turns out, and our submersible pump in the well has been pumping nonstop, creating this fifteen-foot spray at the bottom of our mountain. Fortunately, the house system is full. We switch over to our low-water regime, which means flushing the toilet less often, melting snow for cooking and dishwashing, and sending males out to pee in the bush.

The next three days for Andreas are not only one big maintenance headache, but a freezing maintenance headache. The fuel tank has to be drained, and the filter disassembled, and a new one installed. Then he has to hike a quarter-mile down our mountain with a ladder, pipe wrenches, saws and a heating lamp, and climb down into the well to saw off the old pipe. The particular collar that joins up with the elbow to the main line doesn't match anything he has in his private stock. The hardware store downtown has one, but when Andreas gets down there, he finds that it has a different thread. It will take another day to get the one he needs. Instead, he finds the right collar at a plumbing shop, but by the time he gets home, it's too dark for him to install it, and likely too cold to get a good seal. The next morning he is down in the well again, trying to heat around the cut so that the glue will adhere to the new elbow. Once he has it we'll have to wait another twenty-four hours to see if the glue will hold in this cold. It's anybody's guess.

In part, these crises add to the profound frustration that Andreas is harbouring. He feels that he has spent the last three weeks doing nothing because looking after kids never results in a tangible product, and it takes him away from writing. Even so, these mechanical crises solve a dilemma for him. Miserable as this work is, he feels that he is at least doing something useful. This is the practical kind of caring for us all that Andreas does so exceedingly well. I cherish it. I know few other men who would work so long in bone-numbing cold, when the blood from barked knuckles is too cold to flow. I know he does it for me.

At mid-afternoon the phone rings, and it is Pat, Mum's sister calling from her home at Smugglers Cove in England. "I've decided to come, Sharon. Ted and I have talked it over and we've decided that we can do it and we must. It's frightfully expensive, but I was just sitting here having my tea this morning when my eyes lit upon Granny Oddie's tea service. Do you remember it?"

"No, not exactly. . . ."

"I thought to myself, why not sell it. That's what Grannie would have wanted. So I'm coming."

I run downstairs to tell Mum the good news. She is ecstatic.

"Pat, oh, Pat," she repeats, clutching on to my hand, and pulling my face down close to hers. "Coming to see me? From England? Oh, Pat. Oh, Pat." An hour or so later, as I am fixing her injections, she calls me over to whisper in my ear, "Mother's coming. To visit me. From England. Oh, Mother."

"No, Mum," I explain gently, "it's Pat who is coming. Your mother died about twenty years ago. We lived in France then. It's Pat who is coming." What Mum doesn't want to hear, however, she doesn't. Sometimes it is Pat who is coming, and sometimes it is her mother. My mother, whose hand I am now stroking, has become a child of maybe four or five years. In her excitement, I see flashes of the girl she must have been. Her anchor in the present has been cast adrift.

By late afternoon, Mum has progressed from having her regular cups of tea to having a cup of consommé with a little Harveys Bristol Cream sherry. We give her a wee glass of straight Harveys to celebrate the good news of the day. First, we should have water in a day or so; second, Pat is coming; and third, for the entire day, Mum has experienced no nausea and little pain. We toast it all.

George and Phyllis have just arrived late this afternoon from Vancouver with their daughter Bronwen, who is Sabrina's age. They are laden with bags of fresh fruit and vegetables, Chinese sausage and fresh chicken.

"Where shall I put it all?" Phyllis looks around uncertainly. Every available inch of counter space is covered in unwashed dishes. I had left the ones last night because I was too tired, but I hadn't expected that we would still be without water all day today.

"Dump it on the floor. I'll sort out all this rubble. . . ." I start apologizing. Phyllis cuts me short. "Why don't you go down with your mother? I'll get this in shape up here."

I am grateful. I can use a sag in the downstairs armchair. I give her a hug and head on down. Upstairs, I can hear the bustle of aggressive kitchen tidying. Phyllis is melting snow in the big blue canner on the stove. George is reading a story to Bronwen and Sabrina, and Vanessa is napping. Andreas is still in his workshop getting ready for tomorrow's assault on the well. I nap for fifteen or twenty minutes, luxuriating in being cared for. When I come back upstairs because Mum has awakened and requested a cup of tea, I find the kitchen counters all cleared, and Phyllis scrubbing off the fuzz on my spice rack. "Easy!" I joke. "I'll never live up to this."

She points to a stack of odds and ends on the kitchen table. "I've rooted out the fridge, and thrown out anything clearly rotten or disgusting, but these things look marginal. You decide."

I glance at the stack in the garbage, then scan what is on the table. Phyllis is one of very few close friends who is allowed to poke in my fridge. With most others, I would feel too exposed with things like that tub of yoghurt, stale-dated October 26. I read out the date to her as I chuck it out. "At least it was 1984. Could have been worse."

George goes down to sit with Mum so Phyllis and I can cook together. During the next hour, Mum regales him with all the recent misdeeds of her terrier, the one she had when she was a girl. I pop down from time to time, but he seems to be enjoying himself. Within the hour, Phyllis and I have prepared a four-course Chinese feast. I take Mum down a slice from the bread which I had baked earlier in the afternoon. It is spread liberally with Struan's home-made burgundy jelly. The colour of the glistening jelly is heightened by the liveliness of the fruit border on Mum's wedding china plate. It is indeed worthy of a *Gourmet* magazine cover. Mum eats the whole slice, her first solid food in three weeks.

Her morphine intake is now down to 60 mg every four hours. This seems to be as low as we can go without losing its benefits. She shows no symptoms of withdrawal. Who knows where we all go from here?

NEW YEAR'S EVE

ટ

31 December 1984

Phyllis has cooked breakfast for us all. Andreas has completed the well work, and by now we've even got water again. The furnace is functioning. The power is still on. It's starting to seem that we may be able to make a better start on 1985. Sabrina and Bronwen are down on Grandma patrol, so the four adults are able to sit for a bit of chat around the kitchen table. Vanessa is snuggled on my lap. There are a couple of things we need from downtown, so Andreas and George decide to make an expedition.

"Why don't you guys pick up a couple of ducks for New Year's?" I suggest. "They're on at ninety-nine cents a pound. We can do them Chinese-style."

As they are leaving the kitchen I call, "Do you want to take that FM thing back with you, too?"

Andreas had installed an FM transmitter by Mum's head, so we could enjoy a little time away from her and still know whether she needed help. The theory had been great, but the practice left a little to be desired. When the volume was reasonably low, we couldn't hear enough to determine whether Mum was breathing; however, when we goosed it up higher, Mum's each and every breath echoed off the cathedral arch of our living room ceiling. We cowered underneath. It felt as if the entire house had taken up chainstroke breathing. There didn't seem to be any middle ground. After ten minutes, we turned it off.

Once the men are gone I take up my post at Mum's side, and Phyllis brings her tea down to join me. Robert Bringhurst, Anne Taylor and her two daughters will be arriving later. We had invited them months ago for a New Year's sleep-over, and I haven't felt like cancelling. They will have their dinner at the Elsteds', and come back to sleep in our living room. The Payerles will stay back here for a simpler supper. This is the only concession to Mum's illness that I am prepared to make.

I want life to be as normal as possible. It's the same way I felt when we kept a prior arrangement to have Andreas's family over for lunch two days after I got home with Vanessa from Children's Hospital. It is important for me to grab life with both hands. Never retreat, even if it doesn't all work out.

PAST LIVES

ҿ

1 January 1985

I awaken at 7:30 with the re-
alization that there has been activity going on over my head
for some time now. We had all been in bed by ten last night,
so this is not surprising. I come up to the kitchen to find Robert
washing and polishing last night's wine glasses. The final
drops of freshly brewed coffee drip from the filter.

"Robert! You're a saint!" I exclaim.

"Morning," he replies. Robert never wastes words.

This afternoon I cut up an old Irish damask tablecloth and
sew it into a restraint. The ties will fasten behind Mum's back,
and the flaps are long enough to pin out of her reach. It seems
the only solution to her continued attempts to get out of bed
whenever I am upstairs for a moment or two. A few days ago,
we tried a conventional restraint, but it was too long in the
waist and pressed uncomfortably over her fistula wounds. By
six o'clock, Phyllis and I have dinner ready, and are down in
Vancouver. The men have been having a quiet drink in Mum's
presence. She has fallen into an adolescent infatuation with
George. He is being wonderful with her. They are carrying on
the courtly kind of restrained flirting that I know only from
black and white 1940s movies. I tease her that she is in good
hands for posterity with two novelists and two poets in the

house. Even though I have been working on my parenting book for the past three years, I do not count myself a writer. Not yet. It simply doesn't occur to me that I will be the one to write this story.

George helps me to secure Mum's harness. I tell her that we will be upstairs for the next hour but will come if she calls. She dismisses us with a wave of her hand, but singles out George and whispers for him to come closer. I stop to peek around from the bottom of the stairs. She coyly tries to inveigle him into just untying this little thing here and that little thing there. Only so she can breathe a little more freely. Her flirtatious ploys are those of a little girl trying to wheedle her way with an indulgent daddy. I watch from the stairwell and love her achingly.

Sometimes George is George to her, and sometimes he is apparently someone else. Occasionally he is a cat. He takes it all in stride and purrs appropriately. I find it a great loss that when I try to record exactly how my mother spoke at this time, my mind goes blank. Her speech was peppered with unique idiomatic expressions, and a heightened sense of the absurd.

Once she called me over conspiratorially, and stage-whispered, "You know what would be funny? Just imagine George playing cricket." Then she covered her mouth in her hands and giggled with illicit pleasure.

I didn't have a clue what prompted that, but I found out later that a world-renowned cricket player in the 1920s was the spitting image of George Payerle.

In the next couple of weeks, when Mum called out her delight, she wasn't just using a girlish voice, she *was* a girl. She moved between being a Betty of four or five, a teenaged Betty, a young woman, and a ninety-year-old Betty, years older than her chronological age. For four or five days, the only time she became her sixty-eight-year-old self was when she talked to my father on the phone.

This regression and the actual reliving of past selves is a common part of dying, a Jungian therapist told me some months later at a women's retreat. I'm glad I didn't know that then, because the element of surprise was part of the delight for me. All of a sudden I was introduced to more of my mother than I had ever seen before. I was able to join her as a young woman while she and Pat teased each other about their "men friends." There seemed to have been no shortage of these. The flirtatious shrug of her shoulders and the flash of her eyes transformed her hospital nightie into gowns and stoles. I shared in her delights over bouquets of flowers and the glances of men who were "soft on her." Mother, Pat and I sipped countless teas and sherries together in the late afternoon light of pre-war England.

In time we abandoned the physical restraint because it made Mum so distraught. I relied more and more on Sabrina, when no one else was free, to stand guard.

PAT

۶

2 January 1985

Andreas, the children and I are manically cleaning the house, hoping to get it close to company level clean. George and Phyllis, too intimate to count as company, have packed up after breakfast and headed home to make room for Aunt Pat who is expected momentarily. Mum is sleeping safely in her chair. Andreas is vacuuming the living room while riding herd on Sabrina and Vanessa who pick up the toys, clothes and books in his path. I empty the dishwasher in peace.

The doorbell rings. Here is Aunt Pat, red-cheeked and in her wellies, having gleefully survived the tromp up our mountain. Brian follows with one of her bags. "God, it's good to see you, Pat. You must be wrecked after the flight."

"Maybe a little. You see, it got quite tricky. We were scheduled to fly out of Gatwick, but then there was a dreadful blizzard. . . ." She regales me with the tale of her delays and misadventures while kicking off her boots and shrugging out of her coat. Her accent is sprightlier than my mother's, whose cadence has been flattened by four decades in Canada.

"Let's get the kettle on. Mum's dying to see you." I say this without thinking, instantly wishing I could swallow it. I apologize, but she hasn't caught what I said in the first place, so it doesn't really matter.

While Mum and Pat have their reunion tears and joys downstairs in Vancouver, I start lunch in the kitchen. Vanessa wants juice, Sabrina wants milk.

"Not in that glass, Mummy."

"What glass?"

"The one what has the orange stars."

"Here, you do it." I hand Sabrina a glass and start slicing bread for grilled cheese sandwiches. When the men return, the sandwiches are ready. Sabrina has already finished hers and is downstairs with Mum and Pat. Vanessa is still playing blankly with her sandwich, having barely taken a bite.

"I've got to go downstairs and do the needles and stuff." I interrupt Andreas who is telling Brian details of our recent adventures, with special attention to all the mechanical trials and tribulations. "Here's your lunch. Vanessa's sleepy, so pay attention, eh? Pack her off to bed when she's had enough. Have you got that?" I add the emphasis because I'm not so sure they are listening, "You've got everything?"

Half an hour later when Pat and I come up into the kitchen for our lunch, Andreas and Brian are still deep in conversation. Vanessa is between them, asleep with her cheek resting on her plate and a long slice of pickle drooping like a green tongue out of her mouth.

"You guys!" I exclaim. The two men look at Vanessa as if she has just been beamed into existence when they weren't watching.

"I'll put her down." Andreas scoops her up, and leaves to put her to sleep.

"Men!" I smile resignedly to Pat.

Brian grins and shrugs his shoulders, "Yah, men, eh?"

DRUGS

ė

4 January 1985

This is the second day that we have a homemaker helping us for four hours a day. While Pat is sitting down with Mum, the homemaker cleans up the lunch dishes and gets supper preparations under way. Andreas is up in his study trying to clear all the debris of undone work off his desk when I stick my head around the corner.

"Love, I'm going to take advantage of the homemaker. I'm going to go down and pick up Mum's morphine myself. I need to get out of here for a break. Mum's just had her shots so she should be okay until I get back."

"Are you sure you don't need a nap more?"

"Probably, but I'm too wired. My body needs to move. The hike up and down the mountain will be good for me. I'll take the backpack and buy some milk and another bottle of sherry for the three downstairs lushes. Anything else we need?"

As I head out the door, the rhythms of ordinary life feel luxurious. It is splendid to be able to go for the groceries, and mail and visit the bank; it is my own form of day parole. I walk down the mountain feeling the power of my legs as I swing one heavy hiking boot after another. The snow squeaks with each tread. I've never heard it so cold here. The fresh air tingles my cheeks. By the last turn, I break into a skipping run with my arms fully extended. I am belting out,

"I don't know but I been told,
Streets of heaven is paved with gold . . ."

I feel like a kid, maybe ten or eleven. I used to stand in doorways with my arms pushing outwards against the frame for as long as I could stand. Then I would take one step forward and my arms floated up, all by themselves, with no effort on my part. My spirit these days has been pressed so fiercely against the doorframe of duty that now, even with just this short walk, it can spring free. The colours around me are dazzling; the birds sing with a beauty that aches; the entire world seems freshly polished, newly minted.

By the time I have futzed about for two hours killing time while waiting for Mum's morphine to show up, my joy has evaporated and anger has taken its place. Andreas had dropped the prescription off two days earlier precisely to avoid all this. I pace around the drugstore, reading all the labels on vitamin pills, ointments and first aid supplies. After another twenty minutes passes, I demand to know what is happening. Ten minutes later, I receive a pill container with three tiny 15 mg ampoules nestling on a bed of cotton batting. I am aghast. It is late Friday afternoon and I have been given a quantity sufficient for slightly more than one injection, not enough for two.

"This is crazy."

The pharmacist leans back in response to my tone and volume of voice. I bull onward, "Look here. The prescription said 600 mg, not 45 mg."

"Sorry, that's all we could get." He looks uncertainly around as if for reinforcements.

"But I told you Wednesday how much I needed. If you couldn't get it you should have told me then. What do expect me to do at this time on a Friday afternoon?" I pause and stare unbelievingly at the label on the container. "Do you guys know what you've just done? My mother needs this stuff. Desperately. She's got bone cancer. Why didn't you check it out?"

I am furious, and haven't a clue what to do next. On automatic pilot I drive over to our doctor's office. They are just wrapping up for the weekend when I walk in, drop the ampoules on his desk and ask what the hell I am supposed to do next. He phones the hospital dispensing unit, but it is closed for the weekend too. Gerry, the nurse, phones the other local drugstores. No one has anything. One of the doctors meanwhile digs around upstairs in the attic and comes down with two cards of ampoules from a patient who had recently died. I count them and divide by the number of dosages I need. This will carry us until Sunday night, possibly Monday morning. In the meantime the doctor will call the cancer clinic in Vancouver. It may mean a trip into Vancouver, but at least we will have morphine.

I stride up the mountain with my pack full of groceries, impelled by my furious reliving of this recent turn of events. The hill is long enough and steep enough that ordinarily I would stop at each corner to catch my breath. I don't even pause. My throat is raw from exertion. My fury drives me on.

HELP! HELP!

𝒆

7 January 1985

Jan and Crispin and their baby Jude have come for a traditional English supper: roast beef, Yorkshire pudding, bearnaise sauce, the works. I want to break out of the yoke of duty, have a feast and enjoy the company of friends. Besides I think that Jan and Crispin will enjoy Pat, and I'd like her to meet them. The extravagant meal is because I know how much the Elsteds enjoy a joint of beef, and I always savour their pleasure and compliments. Unfortunately, Mum effectively undermines this plan.

"You're having a party. I want to be there," she whines, an eight-year-old Betty not allowed to join adults at tea.

Crispin and Pat settle her down during pre-dinner drinks while I finish the sauces. Andreas and Jan mind the three children in the living room. Jan isn't ready to visit Mum in this state, but she is not alone in this. Robert Bringhurst, when he visited, also took a pass on meeting my mother, although Ann Taylor and her daughters seemed comfortable enough.

When dinner is on the table we gather around with all the appropriate oohs and ahs, and find our seats. The children have their portions and I am serving the adults when Mum starts kicking up a ruckus, hollering at the top of her lungs, "Let me out of here! I want to come and I'm coming."

Pat goes to check, and when we are all tucking in to our meal, returns to tell us that Mum seems settled for the moment. The quiet downstairs lasts another half a dozen mouthfuls, then resumes at a louder pitch than before. By now the idea of a peaceful meal together is shot.

"You enjoy your friends, dear." Pat stands up with her plate and cutlery in hand. She pats my shoulder comfortingly, and goes down to eat with Mum. I swallow my disappointment. Crispin points out that if we could bring Mum upstairs, she would probably enjoy it. I am sure that he is right, but my anger and disappointment get in the way of creative compassion. Only later that night. when I am trying to get to sleep, do I finally figure out how we could have done it without causing her acute pain. We could have carried her up in one of the kitchen wicker chairs.

The evening winds down early. Jan and Crispin leave. Pat feels tuckered out, and goes to the top of the tower to sleep. Andreas comes downstairs and lies down beside me; I am lying on the covers still fully dressed. He consoles me for the lump in my throat that he knows is still there, and takes me in his arms. I don't say a word. "You're a dead giveaway, Brown. Your nose is all red."

The little black and white television is down on the floor near the head of my bed, and I turn it on with the sound barely audible. The occasional cough and winter snuffle can be heard through the intercom from the children's bedroom. On the evening news, Knowlton Nash tells us in his frank and friendly manner about bombings in Lebanon and the shooting of another IRA suspect. Ironically, international disasters calm me. They act as a counterweight to my personal and private disasters. For now, I don't have to feel any twinge of responsibility for any of them. I just watch them roll past. Andreas hasn't been with me for more than ten minutes when Mum rears up on one elbow and demands, "What are you two doing! What *are* you two up to?"

"Nothing, Mum. We're just watching the news." You'd think we were a couple of teens caught in a bout of heavy petting. I do not have the spirit right now to find this amusing.

"Stop it. Right now. I said stop it! You *are* doing something wrong, quite wrong, and I know it." She heaves herself up as high as she can, but she can't quite see us. "You can't pull the wool over my eyes!"

She is unrelenting. After fifteen minutes, Andreas has had enough. He gives me a hug and heads up to sleep. Steeped in resignation, I prepare the one o'clock needles, turn the television off and am instantly asleep. Suddenly I am startled awake. Andreas is pounding down the stairs into our room. Mum is screaming at the top of her lungs, "Help! Help!"

I leap out of bed in an instant, firmly grasp both her shoulders and demand that she stop. Defiantly, she looks over my shoulder at Andreas. She is enjoying the whole scene. She throws her head back and yells one more time, for good measure, "Help! Help!" I must have been so soundly asleep that I missed the first few yells.

Andreas's face is both ashen and angry. "What's going on here?"

"I don't know, love. I just don't know." I am near tears. Mum looks at us triumphantly, though goodness knows what the triumph is.

"Let's try to get some sleep," I sigh.

RAQUETBALL

❦

10 January 1985

"Child, you're all ruckled up."
Pat wiggles forward on the sofa, the better to tuck in Sabrina's
wayward blouse. She looks over to Andreas and I who are in
the midst of putting on our winter layers. "Be off with you.
I'll be just fine here." She pulls Sabrina onto her lap and reaches
over for the book she has brought as a gift from England. *Moses
the Kitten*, by James Herriot, is the story of a kitten who joins
a litter of piglets to suckle and be warm. Pat is right. Vanessa
is asleep, and that won't last long. I hurriedly lace my boots.

Today is the first day in more than a month that Andreas
and I have had the chance to go off together. It seems strange
to me, as I strip off my winter layers in the women's change
room at the District of Mission Leisure Centre, to see all these
people getting ready to swim or work out. One part of me had
expected the whole world to be on hold just because I was. I
put on my too-tight shorts and my baggy T-shirt, pick up my
racket and goggles and am ready to do battle with Schroeder.

I see him waiting by the courts and take a quick look at
myself to see if I look as weird as he does. Neither of us is
exactly the height of chic. My ten-year-old Adidas are speckled
with porch paint. My T-shirt, with its picture from Andreas's

172

first book of poetry, *The Ozone Minotaur*, is dingy with rust stains from this summer's well water. Andreas's socks don't match, and none of his colours go together. Well, maybe the left sock doesn't clash with his shoes. What the hell. I love him even more.

He serves and I miss. He serves again and I miss. This galls me beyond reason. We are not playing a game yet, just knocking about a bit before we begin. I pick up the ball and whack out a sizzler. He misses. I feel better already. Finally we play a game, and he trounces me twenty-one to three. This stings although I wouldn't normally expect to win against him. He is in better condition than I am, he plays the game more often, and I have been cooped up in one room for more than a month now. I should know it's no contest.

In the second match I give my all and this time only lose twenty-one to eighteen. He has probably eased back to save my pride. My shoulder is killing me. I haven't got it in me to use the rest of our court time for a third match. Andreas tries to read my face, but can't quite fathom or else accept what he is seeing. My nose is red, and I am fighting back tears. I trudge back to the change room. Why should losing a lousy racquet-ball game or two even matter? Surely whacking out all that aggression was the point? Maybe, but as I head for the showers, I'm still on the verge of tears and furious with myself. This is ridiculous. I needed to win. Desperately.

MONEY, MONEY, MONEY

ℓ

11 January 1985

Mum and I delight in Pat's re-
telling of a Grannie Oddie story. Pat cared for their mother at
a time when she was torn between caring for her young family
and helping her husband with his veterinary surgery, which
they ran out of their home. Grannie Oddie lived with them for
years, dying by inches.

"I decided finally that I just had to have a day. Simply had
to have a day, and so I left Mother—Grannie, that is—with a
tinned steak and kidney pie. They were rather good, you know.
You just had to open the lid and then pop it in the oven for
half an hour. So I made sure the old dear was quite clear about
how long, and what temperature for the oven, and we went
off for a lovely day in the country." Mum starts chuckling
because she has heard this one before, although it's new to me.

"Well, Sharon, I came home to find the oven door on the
floor and the most unsightly mess all over the walls and floor,
and Mother hiding in a corner. She was utterly convinced that
the war had started up all over again and was simply furious
with me for leaving her. Of course what had happened was
that I hadn't told her to open the tin *before* putting it in the
oven. It had simply exploded all over the place." Pat's hands
trace a wide arc in the air, her fingers mimicking the splattering

of steak and kidney pie. The three of us hoot with laughter, and she and Mum squeeze each other's hands with delight.

We let the pleasure of the tale linger while the three of us subside into quiet. I play at tilting my coffee cup, quite caught up in the changing light and movement. The surface of the coffee appears to be more blue than brown right now. My mind is pleasingly blank, but the story has clearly taken Pat's thoughts down a useful path, and she sits up straight with an urgency to voice her concerns.

"Sharon, it's hard taking care of your mother when your own children are young. You've got to get help. That's the mistake I made. I never got help. Not that we could afford it, I suppose, but I should have taken her to a home for a couple of weeks now and then just to give myself a break. Well, I did that once, but it was so horrid, I couldn't bring myself to do it again. You have got to understand that you can't go on like this forever. Can she, Betty?" Mum and Pat are of one accord on this topic. Mum nods gravely.

"You can't continue with these kinds of hours."

"Well, no. I guess not," I allow.

Mum shifts her gaze to Pat to see what is coming next. Mum is in one of her more lucid intervals; Pat is right to broach the topic. I am just not sure where to take it next, how to be both kind and realistic. I have tried talking about costs and alternatives with Dad, but I might as well have been talking to a stone wall. "You asked for it," he always replies, with an edge of delight in his voice. When I tell him of any new costs like more ostomy bags and adhesive, or syringes, he is quick to point out, "If she was in hospital, they'd pay for that, you know." I wouldn't mind his bull-headedness so much if we had enough money ourselves to feel a little easier.

Money is a tricky point with Andreas. As a young boy on the family farm in Agassiz, he watched the bailiff seize his father's car after one late payment. At the time, his father washed dishes during the night shift at the Harrison Hotel to earn enough money to hang on to the farm. The milking schedule was fitted around the demands of his paying job. When his entire herd contracted brucellosis and had to be destroyed, it was the last financial straw. Andreas remembers the grey of his father's face at six that morning as he washed, waxed and polished the car so it would be clean when repossessed. Andreas's fears about money are rooted in that time. I respect his anxieties, and find it difficult to do anything that heightens his sense of threat. The bill at the cancer clinic added up to eight hundred dollars a day, all covered by medicare. Now all we can get is thirty dollars' worth of homemaker services a day and the occasional public health nurse or doctor visit. It doesn't seem fair.

"I guess we could hire a night nurse for a couple of nights so I could sleep a bit longer and not have to get up for the shots. The only other option is that Mum could go back into the hospital for a day or so. I could rest up then." Mum doesn't reply to this, but her jaw tightens and she looks down at her knees.

"How much is a night nurse?" asks Pat.

"It varies. I've heard about a hundred and fifty a night. Trouble is, we don't have it. Andreas had planned to write a novel this year, so he won't be earning anything for a while. Our savings are barely enough to see us through the year, and I'm not earning anything." Pat hasn't been privy to our money conversations before, so I fill her in. "Mum had said last summer that we could use her savings to care for her if we had to, but Dad is not so keen. He figures that it's a waste of money."

Pat looks aghast at Mum. "But it's her money."

"I know."

"The old poop." Mum rouses herself. She doesn't know of my talks with Dad about money. "Bring me my purse. I've got twenty-five hundred dollars with my pension cheque in. I'll just write you a cheque." I had no idea that Mum was still capable of any connection with the real world. I bring her purse; she quickly pulls out her chequebook. She hesitates with her pen poised over the cheque, and then passes the cheque to me. "Here, you write the date and amount on it, then I'll sign it."

She scans the completed cheque, and then puts pen to paper. A furrow creases her brow. "I can't just seem to get it right," she complains. She has signed "Betty B. BBBBBBBB."

"Oh, well."

"Let me try again." There is one last cheque. Again, she writes "Betty B. BBBBB." It's no use. Maybe it wouldn't have even been legal anyway. Even though Mum has told me in the past that she would want me to have power of attorney at such a time, we have never put the plan into action. It's probably too late now.

"Betty, it's all right," Pat affirms. "Sharon will talk to David and make him see sense."

"I don't want to go back to a hospital."

"Mum, I'll do everything I can so you don't have to."

"But, Betty," says Pat. "Sharon can't keep on like this forever. We'll work out something."

"I'll talk to David," says Mum. "It's my money."

That night when Dad calls, Pat is down with Mum. I run down to tell her to pick up the phone, and then I run upstairs to eavesdrop with Andreas. We stand joined at the hip in our shared sense of guilt, each with one ear to the phone, trying not to breathe too audibly. Our need to know overrides our sense of decency.

"How are you, dear?" Dad asks with easy concern.

"Oh, I'm getting there." Mum makes the "there" of death sound so matter-of-fact.

"You know, I thought of you today when that Christie cookies commercial came on. Remember the one with the little girl who looks so much like Sabrina."

There is a hesitation before Mum responds, "Yes."

"Except Sabrina is sweeter."

"Yes. Of course."

This time it is Dad's turn for hesitation. "Remember how she says it?" His voice becomes soft, mellow and sensuous the way it always does when the topic is food. "Mr. Christie, you sure make good cookies." Andreas and I stare at each other not quite believing their exchange.

"David? Has my pension cheque arrived?"

"Yes. I've put it in the bank for you."

"David, I want some money for Sharon." There is a moment of silence.

"What do you mean?"

"To get help. Maybe a night nurse. . ."

"Why pay money for a night nurse when the hospital will do it for free?"

"David. It won't be long. We're getting there."

"What do you mean? Getting there? Your cheque isn't that much. What if you spend it all for a night nurse, then where will you be? What will you do when your money is all gone and the next cheque hasn't come yet?"

"Don't push me, David. I'm doing my best. I'm getting there."

"What do you mean? What are you getting at?" He pauses for a moment, but she doesn't reply. He tries another tack. "Anyway, how are you doing? What was your day like?"

In a voice bordering on tears Mum says one last time, *"Don't push me, David. Just give me a bit more time. I'm getting there."* With that she hands the phone over to Pat. Andreas and I hang up, white-faced and soiled by the whole exchange and our invasion of it. This is Mum's last stand. They never talk again.

HER CURSE

ؤ

12 January 1985

The kids have had the flu, Schroeder has had the flu, and now it's my turn. I load the morphine doses for the next two sets of shots, and give Mum her 1:00 a.m. dose. Then I make a mad dash for the adjoining bathroom, and throw up in the wash basin while I'm simultaneously giving my all to the toilet; in the cramped bathroom, the fixtures are close enough together for this to work. After fifteen minutes of spewing, I feel purged but weak. I come back into our bedroom to find Mum staring at me ferociously.

"What's up, Mum?" I say listlessly, not really wanting anything to be up. I am half hoping for one of her old responses like, "Oh nothing, dear. I'm just fine." She says nothing and continues to glare at me. "Let's get some sleep, Mum. I'm wiped."

"Humph," she snorts as she derisively pulls the covers up to her chin. She's not going to quit. I decide to ignore her and lie down on my bed. My stomach cramps ease, and I'm just about to cross over into sleep when I am aware of her crab walking to the edge of the bed in a likely attempt to get up. I am enraged, but go to her feigning patience.

"Please, Mum," I insist, with a touch of whimper. "I'm wrecked. I need to sleep too, for Christ's sake." Mum shrugs her shoulders and feigns compliance. It's a game to see who can out-feign whom. We replay the damned scene at least half a dozen times. Each time she catches me just as I am about to drift off, and each time she responds by either hissing and baring her teeth, or else making a great show of acquiescence until she thinks I'm asleep.

Finally I break. She's got me. I yell at her now with all restraint gone. "Mum, this is not fair! Damn it all, anyway. Just let me get some sleep. You want me to take care of you, well then fine. Good! I will. But I've got to sleep. Two hours even. Then I'll sit you up in the chair if you like."

She is furious. "Don't yell at me like that! Don't you *ever* yell at me like that. You don't care. Stop pretending like you do." She struggles against my hold, trying to get one foot on the floor.

Determined to do what? I don't know, but I am desperate for sleep. I don't care what she wants. I need her just to lie still for two hours. I want to hit her. I don't need her standing up and spilling urine, necrotic sludge and crap on the floor.

"Let me go! I will not lie down. Leave me alone."

"Mum!"

"Don't you 'Mum' me. It's my life and you don't understand a bit of it. You'll get cancer one day. Then you'll see."

I feel cursed. I wish with all my might that she hadn't said that. Anything, but not that. For weeks afterwards, I still feel the bruise of her punch. Everyone in her family dies of cancer. Why not me? She has shot her load with this. We are both spent, two wrestlers falling into one another's arms conceding defeat, but not to one another. I lie her back gently on her pillow and slowly pull up her leg with the cancerous groin. She doesn't flinch, so the morphine must be taking effect. She had been restless earlier and I had given her an intramuscular shot of Valium. I decide that I needn't give her another one. I chance leaving things be, gambling that now she will sleep.

My own rage is still red-hot as I lie down on my bed, rage at the unfairness of it all. I want to give her every inch of my energy—I *am* giving her every inch—but it isn't stretching far enough. Fortunately, my body has its own wisdom, and ignores my rage. I fall fast asleep.

BREAKING A PROMISE

è

14 January 1985

Mum has gone without food or drink for more than a week now. Even when I try to use a needle-less syringe to swish water around her tongue and over her teeth, she clamps her mouth shut to prevent it. She is adamant in her refusal of all fluids. Her teeth and tongue are coated with a thick yellow scale. She lets the Public Health nurse attempt to remove some of that, but fights my efforts rigorously. I can neither understand nor find a way to offer comfort that she can accept. I can hardly get a glycerine swab into her mouth. It shames me. I figure the visiting home-care nurse must think that I neglect her. On the other hand I understand that she can resist me precisely because I am her daughter; we are free to be at our worst with those who love us.

Her last meal was Martin's birthday supper with us. She had turned down her usual scrambled eggs, but happily went for the homemade peppermint ice cream. I had made it with yoghurt, eggs and the candy canes left over from Christmas. Not a bad last supper, since that's how it looks.

I bring tea down and set it beside Mum while she sits in the chair, but she gives me withering glances and says nothing. Her long bony fingers massage her skull as she stares fixedly at the floor. She refuses the tea. Her jaw remains fixed and her eyes retreat further into their hollow sockets. A fragile heap of bones. I offer increased morphine, but she shakes her head. I feel useless.

Yesterday and today, every time I used an alcohol swab before injecting her she screamed like a wounded animal, gripped the tops of her blankets in her curled hands, and trembled. I fear the injections now and have to steel myself for every round. Maybe I should commit her to a hospital. Pat is getting increasingly worried for me. I decide that I need someone to start an IV on Mum.

"Mum, I think we should start an IV again. I know you didn't want one, but it's too hard to give you a needle when you are thrashing around. I am scared of breaking a needle in you or hurting you badly." I pause, awaiting a response. There is none. "Mum, I just can't keep up . . . the way things are." She doesn't move or give any indication of having heard me. Is this betrayal in her eyes? I tread slowly up the stairs to phone our doctor. He agrees to come after office hours.

He hikes up and arrives at our door four or five hours later; we could hug him. Potential rescue is at hand. He greets Mum warmly. She tries to smile, but her face isn't working quite right and she looks away. The doctor, Andreas and I start in kidding one another. He has brought a crash cart from the hospital full of IV goodies.

"Say, that would make a swell box for Lego," Andreas offers.

"Yeah, but my kids have first call on it," he replies, not missing a beat. He asks Andreas if we have any kind of board that could be used for a splint, say eighteen inches by three inches. Andreas returns fifteen minutes later while our doctor is still trying for a good start.

"How's this?" He presents a board of accurate dimensions with its edges all bevelled and perfectly sanded.

"I don't know, Andreas." There is laughter in his eyes,

but his face is deadpan. "It's too good, but I'll try to live up to it."

The energy and banter between them comforts and eases me. I've exhausted myself with willing with every bone in my body that our doctor can tap into a vein and that it will hold. An hour after he begins, he has it. Since we are going against Mum's expressed wishes not to have an IV, we decide on a compromise. The flow will not be sufficient to rehydrate, only enough to keep the vein open. If she wants to rehydrate, she can choose to drink.

MERCY, MERCY

❦

16 January 1985

Late last night, Mum went into a frenzy of thrashing around. For two full hours she tossed her head like a spooked horse. Repeatedly she grabbed hold of the metal headboard behind her. The splint on her arm tore off and the IV needle broke in half. As I took the splint off, unbandaged the wound and removed the broken fragments of needle, I began to doubt my ability to adequately support her until her death.

Mum is living longer than I can bear. Our family doctor stayed a while the night before last, and we talked over what to do next. Andreas and I had been talking about when it was compassionate to consider mercy killing, and we wanted to know what our doctor thought.

He took his time. He talked of cases where it had made sense, and many others where he had his doubts. We talked of the sheer physical volume of morphine that I inject daily into Mum. With her level of tolerance, I suggested that it might take as much as thirty injections to kill her. Using morphine would be crazy, I concluded even if I had enough morphine and could stomach killing her.

Our doctor cautioned us. "Has your mother ever said that

she wants death, that she wants you to give her an extra nudge in that direction?"

These were questions that I had never had to answer in a practical way. Sure, I had a perfectly pure theoretical stance on euthanasia, but this was the first test of where the truth would lie for me, right now.

"Your mother could die successfully at your hands, but you would always live with the memory of having done it. For it to be right, try to imagine what your memories would be." He stopped for a moment. "Sometimes in medicine we err on the side of haste." He paused again, giving us room to respond, but we had nothing to add. "Death, like birth, usually comes best in its own time."

We agreed to take time to think it over, but as I watched the doctor walking out past the greenhouse and down the mountain to his van, I already knew my answer. In spite of our desires to save Mum from further suffering and to shorten our own anguish, we wouldn't kill her. Remarkably, two hours later when I gave Mum the first injection since her one day interlude on IV, she was calm. The stage of hypersensitivity had passed. Perhaps the IV had been worth it after all.

This morning I wash her carefully and slowly. Every day it becomes more of an agony for both of us. For her it is painful; for me there is the unbearable pain of causing hurt. I move her every four hours, although she cries out each time. When she was in hospital and not expected to live more than a day or two at the most, the nurses stopped turning her. Since she continued to live, we paid the cost of that decision with an ugly bedsore an inch or two around, exuding yellow pus from within its blackened borders. As I slowly spread her legs and wash her vagina, I think of how her now-frail body has given birth to, suckled, and mothered me and four sons, now all six-foot men. This same belly that once bore such fruit now bears the seeds of her death, a tumour that demands to be fed from the little life still left in her soft tissue and bone.

As I slowly wash, dry and powder I feel caught in a contradiction: while I want so much to help, some of my actions feel like an invasion. For a while I had used ASA suppositories to control Mum's pain without increasing the morphine. We joked and called them by our childhood name: bum candies. Now the joke pales. The pain of turning her, and the indignity of pushing the suppositories in, seems to out-weigh the benefit. I have returned to increased morphine; Mum is beyond being able to tell me if she agrees.

We expect death, we welcome death and we wonder why it need take so long. Every day I faithfully record her daily urine output. First thing every morning, I lift my head from my pillow and glance over at her urine bag hoping to see such a small contribution that we can cheer that kidney failure has begun. We are like sheepdogs herding her to her death. Every sign of death we cheer; every sign of life we mourn. Surely this is not how it should be.

ENGLAND

17 January 1985

It is Pat's last night here. All last night and much of today she has been wed to the toilet with the kinds of runs that we've all had. She is still on antibiotics for a breast infection that she had when she got here. I reckon she must feel thrashed.

"I'm all right, Sharon. You go and get yourself at least one night's sleep with Andreas. I can keep watch. I'll call you when it's time for the needles."

Gratefully, I go upstairs to sleep in my own bed for the first time in more than a month. Two hours later, Pat is at the bottom of the stairs calling apologetically and softly, "Sharon? Can you hear me? I'm not sure what is happening."

When I get downstairs, Mum is breathing with a strange gurgling breath. She keeps motioning to be sat up, but when we sit her up the pain in her pelvis is so bad that she arches her back and moans to be laid back down. Her throat has billowed out like a bullfrog's so it stands out wider than her cheekbones. She doesn't look like Mum at all. Periodically she stops her ragged breathing, holds her breath for a moment, then hiccups, pauses and starts again. The hours slide by slowly.

"Pat, I can't believe how her body can keep this up. This is awful."

"When we were girls, your mother was a powerful swimmer. She used to make bets that she could swim from the Isle of Wight to the mainland and back again. She won them, too."

We are seated on either side of her bed, each holding one of her hands. *Stroke. Gurgle. Stroke. Gurgle. Stroke.* She's "getting there." Finally, about five in the morning, Mum sleeps. Pat and I slump onto either side of her bed, too bone-weary to move. We doze off.

After an hour Mum awakens, still bullfroggy, but otherwise alert and ready to chat. She announces, "I'm going to England."

"No," corrects Pat lovingly, "*I'm* going to England. Flying to Gatwick tomorrow. Actually, I guess that's today," she adds, giving me a weary smile.

"I'll be in England before you," Mum asserts. Suddenly we believe her.

"Yes, dear, we'll be in England together," says Pat with a catch in her voice. They clasp hands fervently.

"England," says Mum.

SOME BECOME FLOWERS

ۓ

18 January 1985

I switch off the alarm before it rings. My body is getting so conditioned to three-hour injection cycles that it now wakes up all scritchy-eyed in spite of itself.

Mum is still asleep, breathing easily and normally right now, so I take a moment to stretch and wake up with a little more leisure. Besides, I had set the alarm five minutes early. Good thinking. I've got all the time in the world, I think to myself, as I yawn and stretch the life back into my back and shoulders.

Slowly it dawns on me that something is different, but what? I listen with ears and skin on full alert. Same sounds. Everything *looks* the same. Then I realize it's the entire room. It smells quite wonderful with a fruity, flowery scent that on one hand seems familiar, but on the other I can't quite place. I heave myself up on my elbow and stick my nose into the tired hyacinths at the head of my bed; I have been buying them every week as an antidote to fistula stink. It's not them. These ones are wilted enough that they already smell like old mushrooms. There is another pot on the window ledge. Maybe it has finally blossomed. Nothing there either.

I check out the bathroom, but it's not some weird chemistry of the septic field. No perfume bottles have been plundered by little hands. I walk over to Mum who still sleeps, and realize with a start that it is her. I lean over and inhale. This is quite unbelievable.

My mother smells like peach orchards, strawberry blossoms and hyacinths all spun into one. After the smells of fistulas and necrotic tissue, this new scent defies all reason, but it *is* hers. What on earth explains this?

I wait until nine to phone the doctor's office. I had promised to check in, but I also need to know if he has ever heard of such a thing. Is this miracle or medical? I have already dragged Andreas down to verify that I'm not hallucinating. One of the doctors comes to the phone immediately, and when I describe this new phenomenon he knows exactly what I mean.

Apparently, when people are in an advanced stage of dehydration, one of two biochemical chain reactions can occur. One is ketosis which makes a body smell metallic; the other is acidosis, a flowery fruity smell. Some people apparently become flowers before they become earth. Trust Mum.

When Crispin phones a couple of hours later I tell him of this remarkable fragrance. He is silent for a moment, obviously ranging through his encyclopedic knowledge of history and culture. Then he cites stories of this fragrance in medieval tales of the deaths of saints. Obviously they too came to their deaths after prolonged fasting, but Crispin had always thought that the religious descriptions were simply the embroidery of over-zealous imaginations. Now, my mother's dying body is connected in some way to the deaths of saints. As I breathe her in, I feel that she has become ennobled, as have all of us who breathe this air. There is sanctity here.

ROCKS

ę

19 January 1985

I have sagged into the living room chesterfield after cleaning up all Mum's bags, and injecting her 8:00 p.m. morphine. I am exhaustedly hoping for a little respite with Andreas. It has only been two days since Pat left, but we feel the difference already. Andreas has dressed the girls in their pyjamas and tucked them in. I hear their bedroom door click shut. His German folk songs must have done the trick for Vanessa. Finally we have the chance of something like peace and quiet, or so it seems. My heart sinks as Andreas rounds the chesterfield to sit down beside me. After eight years of living together it doesn't take a psychic to tell that he is depressed again. It's not so much what he says or does, but what he doesn't say or do. Tonight his cues are saying "Black, black, black. Leave me alone." This time my concern for him is overridden by anger.

"What's up? What's bugging you? Something's bugging you," I probe belligerently.

"It's nothing."

Not being so withholding myself, I start in on what is bothering me. I can tell by how he slumps beside me that this is not what he needs right now. It doesn't stop me for a moment. "Lover, it is so something. You're doing your damnedest to avoid me. That hurts, dammit." My face is already blotchy, and ready to burst into tears. "Here I am putting out more energy than I have—feeling all this pain—while you're hunkering down in your emotional armour. Goddammit, Schroeder. I need you. I need to blow off steam. I need to be comforted, to be held. I'm spent."

His jaw clenches, and he takes a moment to respond. "Okay. That's fair. It doesn't feel any better to me either. I'm not proud of it. But Jesus, Sharon. I can't go on forever this way."

"It's not forever."

"Two months like these bloody well feel like forever. Especially when the whole godddamned scene is just slammed in on top of you. I didn't think it would be such a long haul. Nothing is getting done. My novel is idling away up there," his voice chokes up, "and I can't even remember what it's about any more." He pauses for a moment, and adds quietly, "I sure as hell am not getting much support or understanding from anyone either."

I keep pile-driving on, "but I can't keep on doing what I have to do with you being so bloody black. I know you need support, and I'm doing my best. I can't help it about your novel. It's not forever that I'm asking this. It's *my mother* that's dying, for God's sake. I need you to *show* that you care." Both of us instinctively know that I am still revving up. The resolution phase, where I can really hear what he has been saying, isn't even close.

"Schroeder, I have supported you in all kinds of ways. For years now. Like when you have needed to go away to write. I've held down the fort. It is your turn to support me. You're getting all skunked out because you haven't *chosen* to do this. I have. These are *my* rocks." I probably said a lot more, because once I get rolling into a good tirade there's no stopping me even long after I've made my point.

The image of the rocks is one we have used often. One day, after we had just finished six months of flat-out building and our tower and greenhouse were just completed, we sat on the front porch congratulating ourselves. We surveyed our domain and idly agreed that someday we should border the yard with rock walls, then terrace the slope. We embraced and imagined future gardens, and growing old together.

Unfortunately, I hadn't then realized that if you put a good idea in front of Andreas's nose, he sees it as a moral imperative. He can't help getting to it right away; immediately, if not sooner. I, on the other hand, come from a family of Irish dreamers where immense plans can be tossed into the air without any serious intention of ever accomplishing them. We hadn't lived together long enough to cotton to the difference. Thus I was both astonished and appalled when I arrived home from work the next day to find a ten-foot pile of boulders sitting smack-dab in the middle of our driveway.

We have gotten a lot of mileage out of that image. We both felt a little giddy with foolishness on that evening five years ago, as we ate our dessert on the front porch and surveyed our boulders. I also recognized the symptoms of a writer's block, and couldn't resist teasing him about it. He took it all in stride.

In this squabble tonight we uncover another dynamic as we clear away our shared emotional debris. Often men feel excluded after the birth of their first child; the love and needs of the baby often lay first claim on the attention of the new mother. These days, like a new mother for her baby, I am consumed by my love for my mother, a love more intense than it has ever been.

Loving which is alive is never static. These days my passion is for my mother, my senses are attuned to the needs of her body and to the beauty there. I ache seeing the curve at the nape of her neck, so emaciated in this last stretch of her life. Her fragility, which terrifies those who fear death, tenderizes me and calls forth my devotion in much the same way that Sabrina and Vanessa once did.

How much loving can we give? Andreas and I talk of what we know, cuddled into each other by now in the embrace of resolution. Once when I was directing YWCA camps on Salt Spring Island, I spent an afternoon on a lichen-covered bluff overlooking the ocean. When I stood up to yawn and stretch, I was overwhelmed by the feeling of being one with the world. The energy from my feet went down through lichen, soil and rock to the molten centre of the earth. My arms touched the farthest reaches of sky. I was One and All.

It was a glorious feeling, one that I grudgingly accept is not so readily available at this stage of my life. Back then my lover was away in Vancouver, and I had a day off, free of responsibility for or to anyone. I was twenty-six years old, in excellent health and with boundless energy. Because only *I* existed in that moment, it was possible for the sense of All to exist within me. I remember thinking at that moment of Walt Whitman's line: "I contain multitudes and contradictions." I know nothing about Walt Whitman's life, but here with Andreas on this particular evening I can't imagine he'd have said such a thing with such clarity if he had been a mother of a young baby. When as a mother I am deep in the muck of life, torn between the need to change my baby's diapers, my mother's bandages, or even simply my own mind, such expansiveness is not available. My spirit organizes a circling of the wagons, a reduction not based upon wisdom, but upon those practicalities which I feel I can handle. A life so reduced is no life at all.

Thankfully Andreas and I are able to hear each other's cries for help, to embrace and to forgive. I offer that if we really can't handle it, I will consider moving Mum to a hospital or asking my brothers for money to pay for a relief nurse. Andreas hasn't asked me to do this, but I figure that I may have to stop being so bull-headed, so much my father's daughter. There is no point in persisting if we destroy each other while doing it.

Andreas agrees that he will try not to care so much about getting things done, but says that he is after all who he is. Maybe he'll just tackle the kitchen floor. "The whole thing needs filling and sanding," he muses tentatively. When I don't object, he carries on.

"You know, we've often got five guys hanging around here just drinking coffee," he reasons. He lays out this plan as if it's just occurred to him, which I'm sure it hasn't. "Your brothers drive all the way out from Gibsons or Vancouver, chat with your Mum for five minutes or so, and then just kill time upstairs. The kitchen floor's about the most labour-intensive chore on my list. We could get started tomorrow."

He jumps up immediately. I know without asking that he's going to check whether he has enough filler. He comes back with two cans and a screwdriver.

"One's a bit dry, but they'll do. I'll have to buy more Varathane though. I'll get it tomorrow."

This is vintage Schroeder, and I feel grateful for him. I know he is doing his utmost these days. "Tell you what, love," I offer, "maybe tomorrow, when the homemaker is here, I'll help you clear the wood that's blocking the road." A couple of weeks ago when the road was still snowed in, Andreas had taken the opportunity to fell a diseased fir, two hundred feet tall. It had landed perfectly down the middle of the road, so that even though the road is now clear of snow, it is still impassable. "Maybe the frost heave has settled enough we could even drive up now if we got the fir out of the way. Besides, I could use some outside air. And I'd like to do something with you. Just you." He lights up immediately, and I am mischievous enough to nail a point home. I figure I can afford it now. "Typical, eh? Rocks?"

Andreas smiles a little sheepishly. We embrace and go to bed, he in our bed in the loft, me down with Mum. For now, life is still possible.

BEAR'S CANCER

ۺ

22 January 1985

It's been a peaceful day. The girls and I are down with Mum. Sabrina sits on the arm of the chair, leaning her head on my shoulder while we get ready to read *Alligator Pie* one more time. We have agreed that I will read the first half of each line so she gets to yell out the second half. At our feet, Vanessa is taking apart and reassembling her Fisher-Price flute. I smile. We had bought it for Christmas thinking that it would encourage her to learn how to blow, one of the pre-speech skills we are supposed to be teaching her. She systematically connects the different mouthpieces and barrels, and then peers inside to compare. Absorbed in mechanical discovery, she could care less about blowing. So much for our speech therapy notions.

> "Alligator Pie, alligator pie.
> If I don't get some I think I'm gonna die.
> Give away the green grass. Give away the sky,
> But don't give away my Alligator Pie."

I pause in our reading for a moment. Vanessa is climbing up on the side of Mum's bed.

"Come on Mummy, it's your turn." Sabrina elbows me.

"Just a second, sweetheart, I don't want Vanessa on Grandma's bed." But I wait without stopping Vanessa, more out of fatigue than reasoned intent. She hauls her little body up, balancing on the top bar of the side railings. Then she leans over with a tissue in one hand and gently daubs a tear from Mum's cheek, a tear I hadn't even noticed. Mum turns her head slightly to see Vanessa. She is no longer physically capable of smiling, but her trembling stops momentarily and she nods graciously, her eyes flashing gratitude.

This is a moment hung still in time. Night after night for the past year I have lain between Vanessa and the wall to buffer her from her heedless head-banging. For hours on end my mind rehearsed bleak futures as she flailed about, as unseeing as a trout in a net. In these sleepless times I conjured pictures from medical texts and replayed parental accounts of the autism that so often accompanies her syndrome. Here, now, today, is the denial of all that: a rumpled tissue in her baby fist, her touch so tender, so connected.

As I hold my breath during her descent from the bed, scenes flash through my mind of what these past few months have meant to our girls. Five-year-old Sabrina drew endless pictures while she kept Mum company as I tossed yet another load of laundry into the wash. Her pictures are pinned on the walls around us. The ones from the cancer clinic visits emphasize medical equipment and overhead lights. The pictures from home feature Mum in her bed surrounded by teapots and cookies. I can hear the pride of responsibility in her voice when, as the delegated watcher, she would call for me to come downstairs: "Mum! Grandma's sitting up. She's going to get out of bed. Mum!"

On the floor Bear lies flopped on a pillow swaddled mummy-like in yards of gauze with a length of tubing leading into a clean empty milk bag. Poor Bear. Sabrina told me with exaggerated and confidential whispers that he had started out with a cold, but it had turned into cancer. Our clear Tupperware lids, now with small brown circles crayoned on them, have become ostomy disks for all the dollies and animals in need. Syringes without needles are lined up for Bear's daily injections.

Sabrina has wanted to be present for everything. She ignores the necrotic stench, though the rest of us still have to steel ourselves against its edge. I can't fathom this, given that she is generally finicky and known to throw up at the smallest provocation. She wants names and explanations, and works her five-year-old tongue around words like ileostomy, colostomy, Ativan and Valium. Two days ago at lunch she announced, through a mouthful of bread and peanut butter, "You know what, Mum? I want to be an uncle-ologist."

"A what?"

"You know. I want to take care of people what have cancer and are dying. They need people what are gentle."

As I replay these scenes in my mind, I breathe a sigh of relief. Vanessa is safely off the bed now. Mum's tremors have started up again, and she has retreated into sleep. The children do have a real contribution to make, and they know it. Sabrina has run and fetched for me. She always holds Mum's hands as I wash the painfully raw skin around Mum's fistula site. She frequently offers Mum candies, not of course missing the chance of one for herself. To moisten Mum's mouth, she offers shot glasses of water which are graciously declined.

As I watch Vanessa scamper back to her rubble of flute pieces, another memory surfaces: Sabrina delicately taking an alcohol swab from its sterile package, and methodically preparing a site on Mum's arm for injection. "This won't hurt too much, Grandma. It'll just be a minute." With Mum's blessing, indicated by a subtle nod of her chin, Sabrina often took on the task of swabbing while I prepared the needles. I remain convinced that Sabrina's involvement has helped Mum to keep finding her courage. Is this a convenient overlay of sentimentality? I think not. Sabrina calls me back from my wool-gathering, "Mum. Mum. It's your turn."

"Oh. Sorry.

"Alligator stew. Alligator stew.

If I don't get some I don't know what I'll do."

RUINED THIGHS

ટ

23 January 1985

Mum is sleeping, the kids are in bed, and I think I'll hit the hay soon myself though it is only eight o'clock. Vanessa has finally fallen into sleep after an hour of sobbing.

"Another day, another holler, eh?" I try for a joke, but it falls flat. We're both exhausted. I slump down onto the chesterfield beside Andreas.

"Hmmm," he replies, and puts his arm around me.

We stare at the fire, too tired to even get up to go to bed. I soak up the quiet and think of Mum. Her injections are getting harder to give now; there is so little of her left to inject into. Many sites are now bruised. This may be because I lack experience, or because every cell wall in her body is losing resilience. Nothing mends now. Her once ample thighs have shrunk to brittle bones draped loosely in wasted muscle and puckered skin.

Andreas and I have so much and yet so little to say to one another. We ache to be together, yet for me to sleep away from Mum is impossible. Even being here at this moment I feel torn. I can't be up here, nor he down there, for too long. The experience when he joined me downstairs a few nights ago to watch television was too dispiriting.

This is as good as it gets. We sit in silence, each in his own thoughts. My mind wanders to which site I will inject next. I conjure up Mum's body, sensing the braille of past sites in my fingertips. I have been moving the injection sites around in a clockwise motion to avoid using the same site again too soon. I picture her wizened thighs with their clusters of bruises. I relive the one time that I actually hit bone and once again I feel the shock of it relayed up the needle. My hand momentarily trembles. In my mind I pat and pinch various injection sites, seeking a depth of flesh that I can use. Absentmindedly, I pat and squeeze Andreas's thigh. Looking down I reflect on how much easier his thighs would be to inject.

He, of course, thinks that this attention is quite lovely. It's been more than a month since either of us has paid any sensual attention to the other. He snuggles in closer with a goofy grin, hugs me and offers a penny for my thoughts. I burst out laughing and seeing his puzzled face, laugh even harder. I can hardly gasp out the explanation about his wonderfully injectable thighs. Fortunately he sees the funny side. We laugh and embrace, and the tears course down my cheeks.

Then, because I had promised to help, and because his need to accomplish tasks never lets go of him, we get out the paint brushes and set to Varathaning the kitchen floor. We start in the middle so that I can work backwards toward the staircase to Vancouver, and Andreas can paint toward the entrance to the rest of our house. As we each paint toward our respective doorways, I follow the sweeps of new gloss in the wake of my brush and feel unaccountably happy.

CRANBERRY PONY

ع

24 January 1985

At day's end, we give the kitchen floor its final Varathane coat. This time I am a little more tired, a little less cheerful than the night before. Part of me decidedly lacks the inner conviction that this is really necessary; another part of me appreciates its importance as a symbolic gesture, a way of showing support for Andreas.

First we paint beneath the built-in table and out toward the kitchen counter leaving a newspaper pathway for me toward the staircase to Vancouver. Andreas will take up the paper and paint the pathway after I go down. It will only take a couple of minutes. Unfortunately, I forget that under the newspapers are two heating vents with their covers removed. I step into the first hole, correct my fall, and stumble directly into the second, skinning my shin in the process. By now I don't know why I have tears in my eyes: exhaustion, frustration, slapstick giddiness, or simply a skinned shin. I wave a listless goodnight to Schroeder, and like an actor in my own play, exit left.

Mum is as she was half an hour earlier, as she has been for the last few days. Her head is turned to her left shoulder with a patch of colour high on each cheekbone. Her arms are drawn up on her chest with her hands curled at the wrists.

Her emaciation makes her fingers look longer, startlingly witch-like. Her pink hospital nightie has sagged on her right shoulder revealing the bones of shoulder and collar bone. I check her bags and dressings. Fortunately, the fistula bag has held this time. Just an hour ago, the bag had come loose and purulent fluids oozed out, searing her skin. It is still red and angry-looking. Her bandages are intact. All seems well. I tuck her in for the night, set up the next round of needles, and idly wonder where I will find enough flesh for the next injections.

After brushing my teeth I sit down, slide my hand underneath hers and hold it lightly. Any movement hurts her, and I am careful not to let the weight of my hand fall on her chest. I start humming a song by Ferron.

> "To lay my head on your blessed arm
> I take my cue from willow tree.
> For it don't break from just one storm
> But bends with a strength that keeps it free.
> For happiness is but a moment's glance. . . ."

I waft into thinking over how today has gone, and what tomorrow will bring. It occurs to me that maybe I was insensitive toward Mum when Jan called earlier in the day to see how things were. I had answered the phone at Mum's bedside. I mentioned that I hadn't been able to find Mum's pulse for a few hours, not thinking that it meant much. After all, Mum has hovered at the verge of death in one way or another for two months now; I've begun to feel that she is not really about to die. Sometimes this makes me angry, sometimes defeated, sometimes resigned. Sometimes, like today, it simply doesn't matter. Jan asked what no pulse meant. I said I didn't know, except that Mum was probably getting weaker.

I talk to Mum now, asking her to forgive me for my thoughtlessness. She squeezes my hand; I am forgiven. I chat a little more, sing a little more, then fall into quiet reveries of my own. I am still cradling her hand when there is a slight rumble in her chest. She ducks her chin as if she were about to burp; then she pales out and stops breathing. Her breathing has been so loud that its absence is startling. The red patches on her cheeks, her shaking and her rigidity instantly disappear. This must be it.

I am pretty sure that Mum has died. At the same time, after this long, I can't totally believe it either. Maybe this is just a new stage. She looks so loose and easy that mixed in with my incredulity is a small spring-fed bubble of joy.

I can't find a pulse, but I haven't been able to find one for half a day. When I lay my ear right on her chest there are still lots of little noises that might be some lower level of breathing. Somehow this should all feel different. I feel disoriented by the absence of any strong emotion. I need to find my bearings. A wet Varathaned floor lies between me and Andreas, and the back door is nailed shut on both sides. What to do next? How will I get him down here to confirm that Mum is actually dead? This is so dumb. And us so good at organizing! Mum would love it.

Fortunately, I hit on the idea of using the phone down here. I dial our own number and quickly hang up. I wait until it stops ringing, then I pick up my receiver and say, "Andreas. Mum has just died, I think."

Andreas is dubious, and asks for details. By now we have to talk over a recorded male BC Tel voice saying, "Please hang up and try this call again. If you need assistance, dial your operator . . . please hang up." We arrange that Andreas will come around to the back window to hand me a hammer so I can pry loose the insulation on the inside of the back door. Meanwhile, he'll crowbar the insulating strips of lath he'd nailed on the outside; that should allow us to get the door open. The BC Tel message loop is still going strong. I hang up.

Moments later, a hammer appears out of the dark at the window. After several minutes' effort, Andreas with a lingering air of disbelief appears on the other side of the door in gum-boots and dressing gown.

We embrace briefly in the doorway and he steers me inside, his hand firmly on the small of my back. We step quickly around to view Mum's face directly. I can see that Andreas is still doubtful. He agrees that she looks different, that she actually looks better. I come around the bed for a better look; she does look better. This is bizarre.

The manic intensity of her stare, the unremitting trem-bling and the rigidity of her jaw have all been replaced by an expression of relaxation and peace. It is now my turn to tremble with a turmoil of feelings; uppermost is relief. We have all made it, it seems, and so has she! We didn't relegate her to a hospital even though it got close. For us, this was the way to do it. Mum was right.

Quiet elation starts to build. Later I will have time for all this to sink in: the importance of letting death take its own pace, the importance of children being involved, and not shut out. For now, I want only to move on to what needs doing next. There are numbers to call, people to notify. Check the time. 10:45 p.m. We'll call it 10:30. It probably took us at least fifteen minutes to get the door open.

I phone the doctors' office and find one of the doctors still there doing charts. I tell him that Mum probably died about half an hour ago, but explain our uncertainties. We didn't want to bother him till we were sure, but maybe he should come up now and do his doctor thing. We had agreed before-hand that whoever was on call when Mum died would deal with all the necessary legal matters. Meanwhile Andreas puts his gumboots back on and troops around to the front door. A few minutes later he returns holding Grannie Oddie's cran-berry pony glass filled generously with the last of our single-malt Scotch. I toast my mother's remains, hug Andreas and grin uncertainly, "This sure beats Cherry Marnier."

PARTING

ؘ

25 January 1985

I waited until nearly midnight last night before phoning family. I wanted our doctor to first confirm that Mum was dead. It seems strange to even question this in the bright light of day, but her descent had been so slow and gradual that it made perfect sense at the time. At Brian's home, Mikolt answered the phone immediately.

"Mum's dead," she said.

This took me aback for an instant, but then I realized: of course, why else would I be calling so late at night?

Mikolt's next statement, though, caught me quite off guard: "She died at ten-thirty, didn't she?"

"But, Mikolt, how do you know?"

"Korina woke up with a dream then. Told me her Grandma had died."

Mikolt suggested that Brian could call Bruce and save me the long distance charges. I agreed. For the next seven hours, Brian walked the streets of Vancouver caught off guard by the depth of his grief. Totally unlike himself, he forgot to call Bruce.

I waited to tell Sabrina and Vanessa until this morning. Blessing of blessings, Vanessa slept through the night, so I've had my first full sleep in months. When she does awaken,

Andreas brings her up into our bed so we can both doze a little more together. When Andreas hears Sabrina awake down-stairs he goes down to tell her the news, then carries her up to join us. She is matter-of-fact about Mum's death. She gives me a warm and generous hug, then asks if she can go down to say goodbye to Grandma. I am not sure about her going alone, so we go together. She walks up to Mum's body without hesitation and gently takes her hand.

"Mum, why is Grandma so cold?"

"That's just her body, and it's dead now, and it's the life in us that keeps us warm. Her life is what's gone." Sabrina continues to hold Mum's hand, pondering this for a moment. "How come if she's dead, her eyes aren't closed?"

"I don't know. I tried to close them last night but they wouldn't stay closed, and it didn't matter enough to me to go and find some way to keep them closed." I pause. "In the movies I've seen them use quarters to hold dead people's eyes closed, but that felt a little weird to me. I didn't think Grandma would have wanted that."

"Can I try, Mum?"

"Sure." She gently touches the eyelids of Mum's body and moves them downwards; when she lets go, they return to being half-open. We stay a little longer. Then I suggest that she go wash her hands and get dressed, and I will cook up some buttermilk pancakes. Times like this, I always vote for food. My mother's family motto was *Ad escam et usum* which loosely translated from Latin means "For food and friends."

I mix up the batter, feeling how light it is to be able to do just that, and no more, not to feel some part of me tugged toward a depth of need that I can never perfectly honour.

I stop stirring and watch bubbles rise to the surface of the batter. A bit more buttermilk and it will be the right consis-tency. Sabrina chatters away to me, and her voice sounds like the music that I am once again free to hear completely. The pancakes take longer to make than the patience of a five-year-old can endure, so she asks me if she can go down again to Grandma's body.

"Of course, sweetie. How about just for a bit?" As the butter melts in the pan, I can hear her down there talking to her Grandma's body.

"Grandma? I'm really sorry that you died last night. I will miss taking care of you, Grandma. Hope you don't feel too cold." As Sabrina says this, I suspect that she has tucked Mum in a bit. She comes up when the pancakes are ready and heaped on a platter.

"Wash your hands, sweetie," I command. "Really well," I add as an afterthought, instinctively expecting dangers from Mum's dead skin. How exactly, I am not sure, but caution seems prudent.

We eat in the dining room, in part because the meal is special to me, in part because I want that little extra distance between our breakfast feast and Mum's body.

The undertaker from Gibsons has been phoned, according to Dad's wishes, in the middle of the night. He arrives, having taken the first ferry, before we are quite finished breakfast. He settles in with a cup of coffee. He is our age and recognizes Andreas from high school. While we eat, he does the necessary paper work and phones our local doctor to arrange for a doctor's signature. Then we all troop down to Mum's body.

For the first time this morning I start to feel out of my depth, although I cannot for the life of me grab hold and figure out why. In my grasping for understanding I feel as if I am listening to a faulty stereo system. Just as a speaker connection can click on and off when the cables only partly touch, so my attempts to think sensibly are randomly blanked into silence. It's as if partway through a song I have to imagine the section that is skipped. I listen as carefully as is humanly possible, but my thoughts won't connect into coherence.

The undertaker wheels in a stretcher through the back door, and snaps it into place beside Mum's bed. I am mute. He lays out a grey blanket, uncovers my mother, straightens her nightie around her knees, gently places her urine bag on her belly, and then transfers her in one easy swoop.

"Do you want her wedding ring?" he asks.

"Oh gosh, I hadn't thought." I look at Andreas but his face doesn't hold an answer. "Yes, sure." As it turns out in her will, she has bequeathed it to her grandson, Conde.

Now that Mum is on the stretcher, the undertaker wraps her up with efficient folds: one, two, three. Even her face. This I am not ready for. I ache for flowers. To have given her one of the season's first daffodils, or a hothouse rose, anything to hold in her hand underneath that grey blanket. But I hadn't known what we would need. The music of understanding has cut in too late.

Andreas helps the undertaker carry the stretcher around to the hearse parked at the front of the house. Sabrina, Vanessa and I go upstairs to watch them slide her corpse into the hearse. For the first time, Sabrina bursts into tears.

"I'll never be able to help her feel better any more," she sobs. "Why can't we keep her here a little longer?"

"Grampa wants her body taken good care of. Besides, sweetie, dead bodies start to smell after a while."

"We could keep her here a day or so. Till she starts to smell. She should get to rest a bit after dying."

I kneel down and hug her, my own tears falling steadily onto her blonde hair. Vanessa nestles deep in my lap. Sabrina is right. Absolutely. What feels so wrong this morning is not the fact of loss—we've been mourning that for months already—it is that we have no ritual to protect us, no known way of proceeding, no connection with our own personal faith and history. We needed more time. It took a five-year-old to state the obvious: that death is like birth. It should never be rushed.

MOTHER'S WAKE

è

26 January 1985

We have held off on Mum's wake until all my brothers could get here. I have been in overdrive all day, cleaning, shopping and baking; my oven has been cooking nonstop. One of the conversations that Mum and Pat and I had, early on during Pat's visit, was about wakes.

"A Lancashire wake, Sharon, is quite different from an Irish one," Mum had informed me. "Pat, do you remember Father's wake?"

"Barely," said Pat, who would have been four at the time. "But I do remember the old-fashioned Lancashire wakes. You had to have fresh linens on everything, the beds, the tables. Fresh towels in all the rooms. Frightful amount of work for the women, but there was help back then. Family help and the servants. We always had help."

"Yes," said Mum, "and you had to have enough food out for two days."

"Two days!" I remember exclaiming. "You mean the party goes on for two days?"

"No, no, no," said Mum, "but people travelled, some of them quite long distances. And they expected to stay with you a day or two before they travelled home. And you wouldn't want to be cooking while they were there, so you made it all it first. Enough for two days. Lancashire pies. . . ."

"What's a Lancashire pie?" I had asked, "Like Melton Mowbray?"

"A little, but lighter. Somehow I think they are better. You serve them hot the first day, cold the second. Pork and ham in them, no beef. Right, Pat?"

So I had my directions. Our pork is first-class, from pigs raised by Ellen and Reg. As I work the herbs and spices into the meat, I shudder as I relive another of Mum's stories.

"You know, Sharon, in our time children were not raised the way I raised you and the boys. We were not expected to understand a thing, not a thing, about how adults felt. I'll never forget Father's funeral. My own father. I hadn't been told a thing." She looked over at Pat, who nodded her head in agreement.

"I'll never forget standing at the side of Father's grave and asking Aunt Molly 'That's Daddy who has died, isn't it? That's Daddy.' And Aunt Molly turning to your Grannie Oddie and saying 'Annie, have you not told her?' And it felt so dreadful being six years old, standing and watching them throw down the earth and just then knowing for sure that it was Daddy. And we were the closest, we were. He would cuddle me on his knee and tickle me and tell stories. We were the closest."

I shape the meat filling into long rolls and place them on the pastry rectangles, wrap up the sides, pinch the tops, and place them ready for baking. Sabrina comes in to help and pats my arm in response to the tears she sees coursing down my cheeks. I will likely hurt my children in other ways. We all do. But not in that way. Thank you, Mum, I think, for giving us a way of dying that even children can embrace.

The guests start trickling in about seven, and extra bottles of wine appear. Martin has brought one of the most recent guitars he has made. It has rose inlays that progress up the neck from a closed rosebud to a full-fledged bloom. It is one of my favourites. By about nine, clusters of people in every nook of our home are filling it with life. I soak them all in, delighting in their presence. Brian has latched on to my Washburn guitar and is serenading the gathering in the kitchen.

"Hey, Martin." Bruce calls out to the living room, "Remember when Dad asked us to sing in church and we pulled off that number? That was too great!" He refers to the time they sang the Rolling Stone's "Sympathy for the Devil" as part of a church service.

Phyllis has just come up beside me where I'm sitting in the kitchen, and touched my shoulder, just so I know she's there. When Brian finishes his song, she reaches over for the guitar, and the two of us sing a song about "ninety-seven men in this here town would give a half a grand of silver just to follow me down."

The songs we all sing are earthy, punchy, sexually alive, vital. This must be what wakes are for, not to mourn death but to reaffirm life, not in a contrived ceremony or carefully honed ritual, but in ragged food and song and drink.

One of our local doctors arrives after midnight after playing his Saturday night hockey game. Later, long after most guests have left, Phyllis and the doctor improvise on flute and piano. Phyllis launches into that kind of breathy overblow that somehow makes a silver flute sound more like blown marrow. Our doctor's head ducks and bobs as he plays. I wonder if he was playing defence earlier in the evening; the thought amuses me. At five in the morning, he heads home, and Brian and Mikolt go downstairs to crash in Vancouver. George and Phyllis haul their sleeping bags to the top of the tower. Andreas hugs me briefly, and heads off to bed.

Suddenly, I am puzzled. How did it all end so fast? Me, I feel as though I'm just beginning. I could sing for hours, at least until the sun comes up. I laugh at myself. Normally I fold long before midnight. The house is peaceful now, replenished with healthy sleeping bodies. The Irish in me surfaces loud and clear. My mother's body should have been here tonight. I had known this earlier in the evening, but the truth is clearer in this aftermath of crumbs and empty wine glasses. I sigh, and start to go upstairs to join Andreas for a few hours' sleep. After all, the children will surface soon. I hesitate at the base of the stairs and smack the banister with my open palm. There is one more thing to do. I go to the liquor cabinet, and into a hand-blown crystal glass I pour a shot of Harveys. I set it on the sideboard for Mum.

Betty Bertwistle Brown (nee Oddie)
1916–1985

ACKNOWLEDGEMENTS

Maryon Pearson once said that behind every successful man there is a surprised woman. By the same token, dozens of people have made this book possible.

June Callwood, who was the first to insist that I should turn my notes on this experience into a book.

Crispin Elsted, whose poetic ear helped me to hear my text and to strengthen certain passages.

Jan Elsted, who is the best listener anyone could ask for and who also endured my countless recitations of early drafts.

Margaret Laurence, who chose my first-born for her god-child, and then encouraged me in all my early attempts at writing.

Kathy McDonald-Smith, who offered me the first opportunity to read selections of this manuscript to a live (and lively) audience.

Susan Mayse, whose editing finesse led me to higher levels of polish and clarity.

Marion Quednau, who, knowing full well the need for quality time to write, helped me with child care.

Andreas Schroeder, whose support in freeing me to write this book has been exceptional.

There are others for sure: Denise Bukowski, Donna Clay, Sylvia Fraser, Joel Ross, and late Renate Shearer . . . my list goes on. For everyone out there who has helped, whether on this list or not, thank you, thank you, thank you.